The Heart of the Global Village

THE HEART
of the
GLOBAL VILLAGE

Technology and the new millennium

William A Charland Jr

SCM PRESS
London

TRINITY PRESS INTERNATIONAL
Philadelphia

First published 1990

SCM Press Ltd
26–30 Tottenham Road
London N1 4BZ

Trinity Press International
3725 Chestnut Street
Philadelphia, Pa. 19104

British Library Cataloguing in Publication Data

Charland, William A.
The heart of the global village: technology and the new millennium
1. Economic conditions. christian viewpoints
I. Title
261.8′5

ISBN 0–334–02438–2

Library of Congress Cataloging-in-Publication Data

Charland, William A., 1937–
The heart of the global village: technology and the new millennium
William A. Charland, Jr.
p. cm.
ISBN 0–334–02438–2
1. Technological innovations—Economic aspects—Developing countries. 2. Developing countries—Economic policy. I. Title.
HC59.72.T4C48 1990
338′.064′091724—dc20 89–48366

Photoset by J&L Composition Ltd, Filey, North Yorkshire
and printed in Great Britain by
Richard Clay Ltd, Bungay, Suffolk

Contents

Preface

In the summer of 1987, I turned fifty and awarded myself a sabbatical. It was not the kind of formal leave one ordinarily takes from an academic institution, setting out to do some sort of formal research. This was a personal search. I needed a new perspective on my work.

For fifteen years, in Denver and Chicago, I'd been helping mid-career adults with educational and employment plans. A former college chaplain, I found adult education a fascinating field. Working with a thousand clients, it seemed that no two were alike. Watching people renew their lives was inspiring.

But gradually it seemed that the personal needs my clients were trying to meet were overshadowed by the social forces they confronted. The economy they were trying to negotiate was shifting beneath their feet.

To choose a career in geology, as many in Denver had, was one thing. But then to find whole sectors of the profession of geology disappear in the middle of one's career was quite another. That was a common occurrence in Colorado.

More and more, I found myself grounding my own work as a career counselor not on traditional theories of vocational psychology but on strategies of economic development.

As a Quaker, I'd been active for some time in an international development program, Right Sharing of World Resources. The committee on which I served reviewed applications and awarded small grants to community organizations in Africa, India, and Latin America.

Gradually I sensed that the same issues I'd read about in Third World development were turning up at home. All of us were grappling with economic development. I needed to understand that struggle better. So I took some time to work and write abroad.

In the course of my travels, I began to change my own career direction again. Journalism had been a great love of mine thirty years ago in college. Now I found myself writing for newspapers and magazines once more, researching and reflecting on the deep social changes I was seeing.

This book evolved from some of that writing – from articles in the *Christian Science Monitor* and *Friends Journal*, and columns in the *Rocky Mountain News* and the *Denver Post*.

But the book is as much personal as professional journalism. It's a journal of my search to understand a changing world, and redefine my own place in it.

It's the record of a mid-life seeker, on the kind of journey many of us might undertake if we could see our way clear to do so – the kind of journal we might write to set down what we'd seen.

Denver, Colorado William A. Charland Jr

1 · *New Vantage*

What does it mean to live through a millennium? With any luck, it seems we're about to find out. I, for one, haven't given much thought to historical eras since I taught a course in the history of Western civilization, about twenty-five years ago.

It was the kind of required course freshmen are "offered" – predigested history. We'd cover a different period each semester, capped by a final exam. This was my first experience teaching and I felt very insecure. I followed the textbook slavishly, dutifully carving up history to fit the academic calendar.

"Now these are the topics to look for in our test on the Middle Ages," I'd advise my equally anxious students. "Study hard, have a good vacation, and next term we'll start on the Renaissance."

But sometimes I'd find myself with an odd thought late at night. What would the people who lived during these times we were studying think of all this? Would they recognize the "periods" in which we'd placed them?

"Wake up, Henry! Remember, today the Industrial Revolution begins . . ." I heard some strange conversations.

I knew, of course, that lived history had never followed the logic of my text. And I especially understood that my own age didn't. I was teaching in a black college in Atlanta, Georgia during the early 1960s, in the heat of America's Civil Rights Movement.

Like many other young adults, I was working in the South to take part in that movement. And the lessons I was learning outside my college classroom were at least as telling as any I was trying to teach within it.

The 1960s were an intensely idealistic time, full of aspirations for justice, peace, and even love. It was a momentous time, suffused with living spirits some of us still have not learned to live without.

But it was a confusing time as well. Beneath all the lofty rhetoric of the day lay some hard choices. People had to decide what to do about the military draft, whether to follow this leader, or join that demonstration. Should civil rights organizations be restricted to blacks? Should a march for racial justice also protest against the war in Vietnam? The 1960s in America were a study in moral dilemmas.

Today, as the vacuous decade of the 1980s expires, the spirits of change are stirring again. It seems the world is teeming with fresh new possibilities. Some of them stem from serious concerns: the environment, political repression, the arms race. Others are expressions of hope and promise: *glasnost* and global trade. Above all, there is an exceptional sense of new beginnings.

The American futurist John Naisbitt believes that part of the power of today's new spirit may come from the approaching millennium, now just a decade away. A common marker-event is likely to reinforce whatever views have currency at the time.

If Europeans were generally downcast around AD 1000, whether from barbarian invasions or the threat of plagues, the coming millennium deepened that gloom. The year 1000 was as good an occasion as any to withdraw from society and await some sort of apocalypse. Many Christians did. And their life-denying values helped sustain the Dark-Age spirits they sought to avoid.

Today, there's an unmistakable countdown quality to the 1990s. This decade may signal our last chance to avert irreversible destruction of the natural environment. As nuclear weapons proliferate, there's a growing concern over conflict resolution, too. Not to mention the depletion of fossil fuels.

There is a moment, just as the future begins, when fate takes the form of decision, and it appears we have a choice. The year 2000 will have that kind of impact. Once again, we're entering an epoch.

As in other periods of change, this one has an organizing theme. It is free enterprise in a global economy. People all over the world seem caught up in visions of entrepreneurship. That may be partly by default. It's possible that no nation can manage a centrally planned economy any more, and that individuals are turning to self-employment in order to survive.

But there's an unmistakable voyaging spirit today as well. Something new is happening. People are investing in their dreams. John Naisbitt, for example, spent years eking out a living by publishing a newsletter on future trends. He had come up with an innovative method of monitoring local news while doing military intelligence during World War II. He found that these grassroots developments were good, early indicators of larger social trends.

Some farsighted people appreciated his insights and subscribed to the newsletter. Unfortunately, not enough did. In the late 1970s, Naisbitt went bankrupt.

Still he held to his vision. He believed that people needed new data on the future, and he had confidence in the kind of information he could provide. Finally, he found new help in marketing from a woman who became his wife. Naisbitt's book *Megatrends* became a best-seller, and he was sought out as a lecturer. At last his message was heard.

People with the same venturesome spirit are turning up today all over the world. Jose Coronas is a middle-aged Cuban refugee who came to Miami, Florida with his family when he was eighteen. He learned to speak English while working in beachfront restaurants and hotels, then went on to earn two university degrees. I met him not long ago in Rochester, New York, where he is a vice-president in charge of biotechnology products for Eastman Kodak.

Jose is a warm, rotund, good-natured fellow – as fervent an anti-Communist as the other Cuban refugees who now dominate the politics and economy of Miami. He told me of a dinner party he'd attended last year with a trade delegation from mainland China.

The Chinese visitor seated next to him peered at Jose carefully, "You look a little different from the others here," he said. "Where are you from?"

"Cuba," Jose smiled.

"Cuba," the Chinese guest reflected. "Isn't that where that crazy fellow is President?"

"What do you expect?" Jose shot back. "He's a Communist!"

They laughed together for a long time.

With renewed idealism comes the return of ambiguity. How much should we trust the camaraderie of global trade? What about the massacre of Tiananmen Square? We struggle with new conundrums.

Several months ago, the University of Denver announced a major breakthrough in international education. The People's Republic of China had contracted to send a large delegation of business and government leaders to Denver for an advanced course in management. It was a promising venture, financially as well as politically. DU is a poorly endowed school, and the Chinese project would bring in $375,000 additional revenue.

Denver welcomed the first class of students – just before the 3 June debacle in Beijing. It's doubtful whether they'll ever see the second group; two of the first arrivals petitioned for political asylum.

That's the kind of time we're entering – an auspicious, perilous age, filled with new prospects and the risk of ambiguity. It's a time when many of us will be seeking new concepts from prognosticators such as Naisbitt, to help us understand what's going on.

But the pace of change today is so rapid that no amount of analytical foresight, not even Naisbitt's *Megatrends*, will do. I believe the times call for a different kind of wisdom, more visceral and organic. We'll need to discern the forces impelling change, not just intellectually but with every sense of our being. It's a time to learn to live with living spirits.

This is a book about some of my own spiritual journeys in our changing global economy. Part of it is set in several countries where I've traveled during the past two years – Canada, Kenya, Great Britain, and various parts of the United States.

The perspective of it comes from the American West, the region of vast, empty spaces where I live. Well, not "empty" spaces; there's a lot going on in the open plains. But most of what's out here requires close attention. This is a part of the world where you must take care to see. It's a good place to look for the presence of living spirits, and to learn how they elude us.

In 1541, Francisco Vasquez de Coronado, the Spanish conquistador, found himself in Kansas. Natives had told him of a great wealthy kingdom, "Quivira," with multi-story stone houses and vast stores of gold. Whoever told him that story must have had trouble keeping a straight face, for Kansas is mostly vacant plains.

"All that there is at Quivira is a very brutish people, without any decency whatever in their houses or in anything," wrote one of Coronado's companions. "I remained twenty-five days in this province of Quivira," the conquistador wrote to the King of Spain, "and what I am sure of is that there is not any gold."

Ironically, however, there was much worth seeing in what is now Kansas. Coronado and his soldiers rode right past a splendid, sacred site of an old native American culture at the headwaters of the Little Arkansas River.

There, in the midst of verdant grasslands bubbling with rivulets and springs, was a sensuous, 160-foot long serpentine figure inlaid in the earth. Undulating along the hilltop, the figure celebrated the source of life in the plains, its arms outstretched to the rising sun and the equinox.

The figure has been restored by archaeologists who have linked it to the vast prehistoric Hopewell Culture whose earthen sculptures are similar to sites around Stonehenge in England. The late R. Clark Mallam, one of the archaeologists, commented: "I think it reasonable to suggest that a 'Kingdom of Quivira' did exist. But it was invisible to the Spanish."

Most of us have just as much trouble perceiving our spiritual surroundings as Coronado had seeing Kansas. For our perceptions of life's spirits are filtered through our values. If we're intent on finding gold, that's all we'll be able to see. Values are the lenses through which we receive and organize life's energies, the spectacles of spirit.

Today's world is a new place for the venturesome. But the pace of change is vertiginous, and it's not an easy place to see. That's why it sometimes helps to take new soundings in the basic currents now forming our new global economy, and reconsider our role in that process.

2 · *Northern Visions*

"Two minutes, men!" The Canadian Football League official shook his head free from his parka as he poked his wind-burned face through the door. He stomped his feet to warm up in the press box.

"When there's two minutes left in the game, if any of you want to try going down to the field, we'll all go together." The official held up two fingers like a peace sign, but his voice was tense as a platoon leader readying the press corps for battle.

"Two minutes left, we pick up and go. Everybody stay together!" he cautioned. Then he darted back out in the cold.

The trip down the aisles of Lansdowne Park probably lasted only several minutes, but wrestling through the reeling, screaming fans seemed to take forever. Buried in the mob, I remembered the shocked expression of a middle-aged lady at Friends Meeting in Ottawa that morning. "The Grey Cup!" she sighed. "Surely you're not going to that filthy orgy!"

Down on the field, I considered what I was indeed doing at this championship game. I was not a sportswriter – only a first-generation American trying to understand his Canadian roots, and curious about Canada's new liaison with the United States.

The previous week, Canadian voters had approved a free-trade agreement with the American Reagan administration. It was a close election, hot with controversy. What would the elimination of tariffs mean to Canada's economy, to say nothing of its fragile national culture! This 76th annual Grey Cup could well be the last, as America's popular National Football League swept across Canada over cable television. Free trade seemed important to the economic future of Canada. But how much of the nation itself would survive?

It was clear that Canada was in for a period of "economic restructuring," as the business analysts put it. In the first phase of a new North American Common Market, the branch plants of US corporations would shut down. American firms now could market to Canadians directly.

Eventually, it was said, Canada would prosper as it found new American markets of its own. But meanwhile thousands of Canadians would lose their jobs. In fact, one day after the election, the Gillette Corporation had closed its plant here in Ontario. Now 600 people were out of work.

In the darkness at the edge of the field, I watched the last plays of the game. Waves of Winnipeg Blue Bombers in gold and royal blue surged against the orange-and-white-clad British Columbia Lions. Two-hundred-fifty-pound players collided in a clatter of helmets and shoulder pads, sometimes crashing off the field into the sidelines as the crowd of 50,000 cheered them on. North American football has been described as "controlled violence." This championship game was especially intense. With sixty seconds to go, it was undecided.

Still intent on the game, I began to sense another, foreboding force behind me. Masses of fans had gathered behind the end zone. They were heaving against a steel fence. Rocking back and forth in a pulsating rage, it seemed they were trying to tear it down. They were shouting something. Twenty meters from me, a gate began to give way. Guards ran to shore it up, shoving drunks back into the stands.

I looked closer at the fans, considering where I would take cover if they broke through the fence and swarmed the field. Most of them were young men. They seemed more incensed than ordinary fans. I listened hard as they stormed the fence, and finally I understood their chanting: "GO GILLETTE, GO! GO GILLETTE, GO!!"

"Economic restructuring" is one way to describe the transition under way in Canada. As I traveled across the country I often heard that kind of analysis on the CBC. The Canadian Broadcasting Corporation is one of the premier radio networks in the world. Like the US National Public Radio, the CBC specializes in sprightly social commentary. Like the British Broadcasting Corporation, its programs are available round the clock. But the CBC enjoys the unique advantage of broadcasting across a vast, open land where many listeners have few distractions. The Canadian network can probe issues at depth.

Driving thousands of miles among the football franchises of Canada, I heard plenty of economic analysis on the CBC. With free trade debate in the air, the broadcasts offered a short course in labor economics. Canadians are a thoughtful lot, and some of the economists' terminology had a familiar academic ring. Like "economic restructuring." Or "dislocated worker."

"What we have here in southern Ontario is a case of economic restructuring, with a consequent population of dislocated workers," a labor economist might observe. Then he'd outline some strategies to address the problem: income subsidies, retraining programs, early retirement, relocation.

Out in the wilderness of Manitoba, this kind of analysis did me good. Driving through a stand of pine trees past a black bear with her cubs, watching out for moose, I began to get the big picture on the US free trade agreement.

In Saskatchewan, I learned about the economics of potash in foreign trade. One could see the huge potash-processing plants on the far horizon. Long and sprawling, miles from the highway, they appeared to be belching dust or smoke. Potash, I learned, is a fertilizer found naturally in the soil of Saskatchewan but only rarely in the United States. Canada supplies more than eighty per cent of the potash delivered to the US. The Soviet Union is another, less reliable, supplier.

Only four per cent of the potash consumed in America is produced domestically, mostly from a couple of mines in New Mexico. Neither is much of an operation. One went bankrupt recently, its agribusiness owners indicted for fraud. But the potash producers had close ties to the Reagan administration. Their lobbyists sought special duties on potash imported from Canada, to protect the price of their own product.

These "dumping penalties" threatened Saskatchewan's economy in particular (potash plants were the only manufacturing facilities in the province of any size). They also presaged other protectionist legislation brewing in Congress. Canadian officials were worried. They quickly proposed trade talks to shield other industries from arbitrary US trade restrictions.

But the free-trade discussions opened a Pandora's box of Canadian fears. They highlighted all the painful disparities of Canada's coexistence with a neighbor ten times its size. Two-thirds of Canadian exports go to the United States, and two-thirds of its imports come from there. The US market accounts for twenty to twenty-five per cent of Canada's wealth, the Canadian market less than two per cent of America's. Finding one's way in a market that size was no easy matter.

All of this reflection provided the kind of perspective and distance from Denver, Colorado that I needed. The late 1980s decline of oil prices and OPEC had placed me in a professional double bind. My practice at the University of Denver was booming. I was counseling more unemployed geologists than I could count and making a good living from their fees. My only problem was that I'd run out of ideas on other work they might do.

Denver lost 50,000 energy-related jobs in three years. Most of those were high-paying professional positions, and the loss of that spending power reverberated throughout the local economy. Businesses closed, office vacancies soared to the highest rate in the nation, the symphony orchestra folded. Our miseries compounded.

I became more and more dissatisfied with the kinds of services career counselors had to offer, including my own. I'd done everything I could think of to help my hordes of newly unemployed clients. But administering vocational interest tests and preparing attractive resumés don't always help people who've lost their jobs. Not if there's no alternative employment. One day I decided I needed a break from the whole scene.

My wife Phoebe and I had considered doing some overseas work. Was this the time for that? I'd also begun to develop an interest in my late father's ancestry, after my son had taken a course in Canadian history. As an incurable sports fanatic, I'd had a long fascination with the Canadian Football League.

One summer day, Phoebe and I were sitting in the back yard, talking. It was one of those quiet afternoons just right for daydreaming, and I found myself with an unexpected fantasy. "Here's what I'd really like to do," I heard myself saying. I wanted to try my hand at some other kinds of writing: maybe travel writing, like one of my favorite authors, V. S. Naipaul. Then another wish surfaced: I've always wanted to see a Canadian Football League game. Maybe I could try writing something on the CFL. "Why not?" asked Phoebe. I couldn't think why not, so I did.

Now here I was in Canada, ostensibly to relax and try my hand at travel writing. Yet I found it somewhat difficult to escape. I kept encountering similarities between Canada and Colorado. Many of the problems they faced and the solutions they were considering seemed the same. And I found myself continuing to come up against the impact of economic change on the lives of real people.

Jack is an American friend of mine from college who now manages a family business in Toronto, a philosophy major who went on to the Peace Corps. I remember when he first began considering prospects with a family business owned by a Canadian uncle. (Americans and Canadians are so interrelated that it seems that almost everyone on one side of the border has a relative on the other.) I never expected that he'd end up in business. But he enrolled in an MBA program at the University of Chicago and joined the family firm in Toronto. Now he's a Canadian citizen. He is also one of the brightest businessmen I know.

I sat up late a couple of nights and talked with Jack about the impact of free trade on his business. His firm distributes a dozen barber-shop and beauty products throughout Canada. Some of the products are made in Toronto and others through affiliates in Illinois.

It is clear now that the business of serving as a Canadian distributor will soon be over. Jack's firm will have to select two or three product lines in which they can excel, and try to establish a market for them throughout North America. He voted for free trade for philosophical reasons, but the measure will complicate his life. Which products should the company develop? He ponders that question a good deal, as his sixteen-year-old daughter worries about funds for college.

Jack's case brought the notion of "economic restructuring" into sharp focus. I saw some reasons for optimism about it: long-term benefits of free trade to certain sectors of the Canadian economy. I also recognized how many industries in the Western provinces needed trade protection. And I knew that in some industries Canadians already were marketing specialized skills throughout the world – wilderness engineering, parlor games. (*Trivial Pursuit* was the first of a whole run of best-selling board games in the US that were conceived in the cold winters north of the border.) And of course I had confidence in my friend.

But there were other downside factors. Some analysts were convinced that free trade was nothing but a smokescreen for the interests of multinational corporations. A single North American economy was easier game for the multinationals. And what about the Canadian businesses that weren't large enough to compete across the continent, or lacked well-trained leaders such as Jack? Not to mention the workers who didn't own a business, but counted on a company like Gillette?

I remembered all the unemployed young people I'd seen hanging out in coffee shops in the Western provinces. The energy industry collapse had been every bit as damaging there as in Denver. And the ramshackle hot dog stands with the remnants of roller-coaster rides that littered the shoreline in Vancouver, British Columbia. Two years ago, they'd put on an exposition to lure new business into the area as the lumber industry declined. The exposition had suffered heavy losses, and unemployment still topped twelve per cent in many sections of the West.

In Colorado or Canada, by whatever name, economic restructuring was a tough experience to live through. For most people it translated into plain hard times. I couldn't forget the cries of the crowd in Ottawa: "GO GILLETTE GO!!" Or the pathetic graffiti I found scrawled on a downtown wall. It was spray-painted black in two-foot letters: "SOMEBODY GET ME A JOB."

3 · *Global Forces*

As it turned out, there was no escaping the US up in Canada. The free-trade debate spotlighted some serious questions looming in the American economy. Traveling throughout Canada, I found that one could see many facets of life in the United States more clearly from there.

A companion culture to the US, Canadians attend to their larger neighbor as carefully as the Scots do to England. With a common language and similar culture, very little is lost in translation. Canadian Prime Minister Pierre Trudeau once compared life with the United States to sleeping with an elephant: in Canada, one felt every grunt and twitch.

Clearly, the free-trade agreement or something like it was inevitable. Just as European countries purposed a genuine Common Market in 1992, Canada seemed to need a larger marketplace as well. North American free trade was just one current in a larger movement toward a more integrated global economy. A few ideologues like Margaret Thatcher might quibble over terms of the process, but the move to international trade seemed inexorable. Free trade was not an option Canada could ignore.

But the condition of the US economy signaled caution. Should Canada hitch its wagon to a falling American star? The Canadian press simmered with misgiving. One editorial cartoon portrayed a little Canadian beaver handcuffed to a large American eagle, plummeting to earth with a foolish grin.

There was a good deal about the US labor economy to give pause.

America was steadily losing manufacturing jobs, for one thing. In 1929, forty-five per cent of American workers were employed producing goods. In 1977, that figure was thirty-two per cent. It was twenty-five per cent in 1986.

From one perspective, this shift in the nation's economy didn't look bad. Some analysts maintained that America was simply passing through an economic restructuring like that of Great Britain. Mass production manufacturing was moving overseas, to low-wage Third World nations. The new US role seemed to be in computer-supported, customized manufacturing. America was in transition, on the road to a new high-tech economy, making things for "niche markets."

One could see evidence of this trend in old manufacturing centers such as Pittsburgh, Pennsylvania. Pittsburgh suffered through a couple of horrendous decades as the steel industry moved south to Birmingham, Alabama, and overseas to South Korea. But the city's excellent universities were a trove of research and development. The schools had produced a whole new generation of advanced technology. Now there were more new jobs in small, customized, computer-supported manufacturing facilities than had been lost from the massive steel plants.

In addition, one could argue that America's new "service economy" was generating record numbers of jobs – manufacturing aside. If one simply tabulated numbers of jobs lost and gained, it seemed possible to see those who had lost their jobs as "dislocated" rather than unemployed. Vocational counselors took to this kind of analysis. Their journals were full of "life adjustment" programs that taught people how to dress up and interview for new jobs. After all, the jobs were out there. America and its workers would be all right. We were just working through a period of transition.

But others in Canada and the US saw serious problems in the kinds of jobs America's new economy was creating. In 1989, the nation's top four employers were two fast-food restaurant chains: McDonald's (1) and Burger King (3), the Federal Government (2) and a retail chain: Sears Roebuck (4).

Middle-income employment had fallen from seventy-five per cent of American jobs in 1963 to thirteen per cent in 1988. This shift coincided with an eighty per cent reduction in federal housing appropriations during the Reagan administration. On any given night in America, three million people were living on the streets.

Two sociologists at Temple University in Philadelphia devised an ambitious study of homeless people in the state of Pennsylvania. On the night of 28 January 1989, they arranged a survey of every homeless person in the state. The study turned up some startling insights into the homeless population, contradicting some common stereotypes.

In the popular view, most vagrants suffer from mental illness or an addiction of some sort. But the Temple researchers found that two-thirds of the homeless were not alcoholics or drug addicts. And seventy-five per cent of them were not mentally ill.

The largest group of homeless were young adult males. But a quarter of them were families (usually single parents) with children.

Perhaps the most remarkable finding was that forty per cent of Pennsylvania's homeless people were currently working or had recently been employed. Other research confirmed the same pattern. A random sample in Denver found that sixty-five per cent of the homeless had been employed within the past six months.

America, it seemed, was engendering a new social class, the "working poor." With an unraveling economy and the weakest system of social supports of any developed nation, many Americans were losing their homes while still employed.

Was this indeed a transition we were seeing, or just a plain and simple downward spiral? Paul Kennedy, a British-born historian who taught at Yale, came out with a timely book on empires in decline. It was a ponderous book, full of footnotes for the benefit of other historians. One could hardly imagine many ordinary readers plowing through it. Yet, *The Rise and Fall of the Great Powers* became a best seller.

Kennedy's thesis struck a chord. The United States, he maintained, is in a long period of reaction to imperial over-reach. Just as Britain before us, since World War II we've dominated the world economy out of all proportion to our size, and far past our time. Vietnam was our last imperial adventure. Now we must learn to live within our means as we enter a slow but inexorable history of decline.

For a while, *The Rise and Fall* triggered vigorous debate. But the thesis seemed unsatisfying in the long run. Something about the American character resists passive self-perceptions such as the School of Decline. Americans are pragmatic problem-solvers, and activists at heart.

It seemed to me that Kennedy's views had merit, on moral grounds for one thing. I'll always remember a quote from *Taking Charge*, a publication by a group of Quakers living collectively in San Francisco.

> If the world were a global village of 100 people, six of them would be Americans. These six would have over a third of the village's income, and the other 94 would subsist on the other two-thirds. How could the wealthy six live "in peace" with their neighbors? Surely they would be driven to arm themselves against the other 94 – perhaps even to spend, as Americans do, about twice as much per person on military defense as the total income of two-thirds of the villagers.

Yet, as a product of American culture, I was too much an activist to find contentment feeling guilty. Kennedy's decline theory smacked too much of "the paralysis of analysis," the theorizing of tired civilizations. It seemed to me we'd already been handed too many concepts that didn't fit us.

Ever since World War II, it seems our universities have echoed with the ruminations of exiled European intellectuals. These brilliant and sensitive social analysts have taught us to see history as a series of disjunctive episodes whose meaning can be grasped, if at all, only after the fact. "We live in a time when one age has died and the other is powerless to be born," said Hannah Arendt of the University of Chicago.

Perhaps that's why so much of our literature on economic change has had such a tentative tone, focused on what the coming economy is not. We've been guided by slogans such as the "post-industrial society" of Daniel Bell, the vague "Third Wave" of Alvin Toffler, and psychologist Jean Houston's comment that we live in "the time of the parentheses."

Many of us have become functional existentialists as well, drifting past basic decisions of our economic life as though lost in a kind of narcosis. In the past decade, America has continued to consume goods we do not produce and can no longer afford. For the affluent, the Reagan years were a fat man's picnic.

That's how we have fallen from the largest creditor to the largest debtor nation in the world, more and more in the thrall of others. When Ronald Reagan took office in 1980, direct foreign investment in the United States amounted to $90 billion. When he left office in 1988, the figure was $304 billion.

Suddenly, it seems we can no longer tolerate the time of the parentheses – punting along in the fog of someone else's history. It seems that we find ourselves in the strange craft of a new global environment – carried along on a current that is rapidly picking up speed.

Now the ride seems less like a rowboat and more like a whitewater raft. Languid musings on decline seem absurdly self-indulgent and defining our times by the scenery we've passed is no longer enough. Most of us recognize we're in some peril together. We need a better view downstream.

Back in Denver, I found myself restive for something effective to do – a career counselor with questions of my own. Part of the answer came in the form of a new avocation. Through an article I'd published on the Canadian Football League, I came to the attention of a local newspaper, *The Denver Post*. I was asked to do an article on employment in Colorado, then offered a column on emerging careers.

I enjoyed the activity of journalism, researching new occupations and training opportunities. Gradually I recognized that many of the listening skills I'd developed in counseling also were useful in writing. It was an ability I enjoyed using – helping people feel comfortable talking about themselves.

The subject-matter was satisfying, too. Tracking new careers felt more satisfying than simply analysing social change, especially the kinds of change we were seeing.

Of course, I recognized that any attempt to forecast changing trends was hazardous at best. American futurists were notoriously superficial. In *Megatrends*, John Naisbitt advised Americans to migrate to "Ten Great Cities of Opportunity" in the Southwest, notwithstanding that they may soon run out of water. "Brazil is the next America," he proclaimed in a Denver speech last year – even as the Brazilians were leveling their rain forests.

Still, it pleased me to fancy myself a futurist, as fallible as the rest. Depicting the future was a take-charge sort of literary venture.

But it wasn't quite active enough. I still hoped that one of the inquiries I'd sent out for overseas work might materialize. I needed an opportunity to offer some different kind of service in another place. And I still was groping for a larger perspective on life in my own land.

Eventually, a way opened. I was asked to spend a month in Kenya and seized the chance to go back to Africa. The assignment was working with the faculty of a two-year technical training institute, studying their needs as a basis for some long-term development work. Friends College Kaimosi was a Quaker institution that had been founded in the first enthusiasm of Kenyan independence. Since then, relationships with Friends in other parts of the world had broken down.

Phoebe and I had visited this school while attending a conference six years before. We'd enjoyed getting to know several people in the local community and gaining some exposure to their culture. Now perhaps I could help the school.

I didn't anticipate how much the Kenyans and others I met in other countries would help me in return. In a new sphere of distance from Denver, I found a larger vision of the world.

Traveling and talking with many kinds of people, I began to see beyond the between-times rhetoric I'd read for so long. It came to me that the currents shaping today's changing global economy actually can be seen. There are three strong forces at work. Each is powerful in its own right, capable of initiating change. But the combined effects of advanced technology, resource constraints, and instant communication are incredibly powerful. They're swirling in a compelling tide that has the whole world in its sway.

New technology was everywhere, from Swiss Informatique computer shops to Silicon Glen in Scotland. Not that technology is a new invention. Human beings have always been coming up with new devices. Prehistoric sites are littered with tools. "What do you suppose they used this for?" is a basic question in archaeology.

But I could imagine a career in archaeology many centuries from now. How could scientists begin to make sense of the numbers of thingamajigs we're coming up with? Computer science, biotechnology, telecommunications, and advanced materials were intersecting in a giant, conglomerate, multiplier effect.

Researching my careers column, I had some close-hand glimpses of new products. I spent an afternoon at US WEST Advanced Technologies, a telecommunications research facility in Denver. In four years the new division has grown from eight employees to 450. These researchers are working on twenty-eight different technical projects, each of which represents a potential new product.

Naturally some of the inventions are secret. But three of them are public knowledge, clearly headed for the marketplace. One of them is the home information center.

Information Gateway is similar to the Minitel videotex system now widespread throughout France. Gateway currently is being test-marketed in Omaha, Nebraska – a mainstream Midwestern city well-suited to studying conventional tastes.

Gateway is the electronic telephone directory of the future, and a good deal more. All kinds of information, from financial news to restaurant guides, will soon be available in American homes through a small electronic unit like a hybrid telephone/computer.

The video phone is another emerging product. This device was conceived years ago; the technology has been available for decades. Now the costs of video transmission are coming down at a rate of fifty per cent each year. US WEST employees are already testing the video phone, collaborating across phone lines among distant cities. The demonstrations I've seen still look crude. Engineers shout into their telephone speakers and squint at wall charts that look miniscule on video terminals.

But the video phone is on the way. Within five years, grandparents will call and see their offspring. Telephone solicitors who "cold call" selling stocks and bonds during dinner will be recognized as unfamiliar faces. "Telemarketing" does not strike me as an occupation of the future.

Already, in fact, a "custom ringing" telephone system is being tested in Colorado Springs, Colorado. The system provides friends, relatives, and other frequent callers with a special distinguishing ring.

The other innovation I saw was particularly intriguing. It is an interactive system to provide travelers with local information. The new telephone/computer device is housed in a touch-screen kiosk. (Instead of punching keys, one touches a label on the video screen; a heat-sensor transmits the message.) "Info-To-Go" was test-marketed in Vail, Colorado, this winter during the world alpine ski championships. Visitors to the ski resort received an instantaneous overview of restaurants, lodging, and other facilities.

A similar device has been developed for Newport, Rhode Island – a popular East Coast American tourist center with many attractions concentrated in a small space. A Scottish computer firm has developed an electronic map of the island resort based on "hypermedia," computer technology that compares and correlates information.

Now visitors need no longer fumble through racks of pamphlets to find the places they want to see. Each person can designate his or her special interests and receive maps and in-depth information on just those attractions.

Innovation in high technology links today's industrialized countries, often in competition. Americans are obsessed with the threat of Japanese technology, but invention is ubiquitous. A major competitor of Info-To-Go, the US WEST interactive video kiosk, is OWL of Scotland: a hypermedia firm from Silicon Glen.

The pace of innovation is phenomenal. Hewlett-Packard, an American computer manufacturer, earned half its income in 1988 from products less than two years old.

What is driving all this technological change? I don't believe it's that we industrialized humans have suddenly got smarter, though we certainly are accumulating vast stores of information. Nor is it that we seem to need a new technology every once in a while to juice our economy, though there's something to that as well. Basically, I believe, our investment with advanced technology stems from environmental fears.

From the tragedy at the nuclear plant of Chernobyl, to the Exxon tanker's horrendous oil spill in Alaska, to whatever debacle comes next – the media are full of reminders that we're long overdue for a new, less threatening lifestyle. The heavy manufacturing era we have just been through hasn't lasted a long time. The oil industry, for example, is less that 150 years old. But it's been the most noxious industrial era in history.

Now the unparalleled consumption of natural resources in the industrialized nations is spilling over into developing countries. There its consequences may be even worse.

In Brazil, Naisbitt's "new America," ten per cent of the nation's tropical rain forest has been destroyed within the past five years. According to Jack Cox who traveled there last year for the *Denver Post*, "If the deforestation continues at the current rate – equivalent to the loss of one soccer field every five seconds, or five Yellowstone Parks each year – many scientists fear it could heighten the 'greenhouse effect' . . . the worldwide buildup of air pollutants that absorb the sun's rays and may be triggering a global warming trend."

Scientists warn that the loss of irreplaceable rain forest brings with it the destruction of countless forms of life. In one thirty-mile section of the forest, Cox found, "researchers have counted more than 300 species of birds – nearly half as many as are found in the entire lower forty-eight states. They've also identified more than 300 species of trees – ten times as many as would typically be found in a patch of North American forest the same size."

In addition to its natural face value, the abundant life of this area contains a wealth of medicinal and other new materials which could be refined through the emerging science of biotechnology. "Its curare vines," Cox writes, "yielded a muscle relaxant that was administered to former President Reagan, and its bushmaster snakes produce a venom that led to the development of a potent new drug to control high blood pressure."

Brazil's environmental holocaust has a great deal to do with local conditions: a seventy-three per cent urban population, and per capita income of $2400 per year. The Amazon rain forests represent the same kind of open frontier Americans scavenged in the last century, and the same scramble for survival that sacrifices 70,000 African elephants every year for the black-market value of their tusks.

But other dimensions of the problem are global. The rush to development in Brazil stems from desperate economic relations with developed countries – the rush to raise beef on deforested ranch lands for American fast food chains; the burden of interest payments on Brazil's $120 billion foreign debt.

And in the final analysis, the consequences of deforestation are global. Life will be altered all over the earth. Soviet former foreign minister Anatoly Gromyko asks: "When in human history . . . have we had such clear evidence that we humans have arrived at a limit?"

High-tech industries seem to offer an alternative to this devastation, for they are not energy-intensive. Naisbitt estimates that the fossil-fuel requirements of electronics manufacturing are only one per cent of heavy industrial manufacturing.

One can see evidence of how few natural resources high-tech firms require throughout the American Southwest. Albuquerque, New Mexico, sits at the base of a mountain range on the Rio Grande River. The region is essentially a desert. Most of the year the Rio Grande is barely a trickle.

Yet the city has marketed itself successfully to high-tech manufacturers in northern California's overcrowded Silicon Valley. Several large branch plants now manufacture computer chips on the barren outskirts of Albuquerque. High-tech industries require well-trained work forces and good transportation and communications networks. They don't need much water, petroleum, gas and coal.

Every environmental disaster of the passing industrial culture promises to accelerate high-tech research and development, strengthening our search for a new benign economy.

In all my travels, I've never quite got over the third global force I found in the new economy: our unprecedented communications capability. Marshall McLuhan, Walter Ong, and other communications theorists predicted the coming global village decades ago. I appreciated their image but didn't think much about it till an experience several years ago in a traditional native village of East Africa.

I was visiting friends in a remote area of Kenya. After dinner we sat round the mud-floor living room, visiting by the dim light of a kerosene lamp. A steady rain beat down on the sisal roof.

Suddenly, this rustic scene was transformed. The eldest son left the hut for a moment and returned with a short-wave radio. He tuned in a West German station, and for the next hour we listened to a review in English of a Pan-African Congress in Libya. The global village had arrived.

Last summer on a layover in Switzerland, I awoke to the sound of a radio from the next room in the hotel. Something about the songs seemed incongruous. Gradually, as I shook off my jet lag, it dawned on me that this was the same popular music I'd heard at home. Later I'd have the same sense in Scotland, listening to jokes about (English) Yuppies way out on the Isle of Skye.

The same popular culture extended to Kenya. On the streets of Nairobi, I heard some trenchant reviews of Hollywood films.

"Hey, what's this Rambo III about?" one African asked another.

"You remember Rambo II? It's about one homicide a minute."

Most of the American hits played in Nairobi. So did the worst of television sit-coms, from Britain as well as the US.

Even home videos were flourishing. An editorial cartoon in a Nairobi newspaper portrayed a Kenyan police official leaning over the counter of a video store, pointing to a wall stacked with films. "Come of (sic) it, Man," the official glowers. "Of course I know they are phonographic (sic). I have seen them all!" (The cartoonist's halting English still beat my Swahili.)

Even in the outback of Kenya's Western Province, popular culture followed. We stopped for provisions at an open-air market in Kisumu, a small city on the shores of Lake Victoria, on the way to Friends College. I stood outside the market to wait, a lone Caucasian "mzungu" in a sea of black shoppers. Soon I was surrounded by street peddlers; I'd expected that.

What I hadn't foreseen was the tape cassettes of American musicians they were prepared to sell me – Don Williams, Dolly Parton, to say nothing of the rock stars. I stood there under the palm trees and pondered: "In all the world, one cannot escape Country Western Music or Madonna."

Even out in the rain forest of Kaimosi, where they have ten-foot black mamba snakes and monkeys in the trees, the same popular culture persisted. A young farmer walked by in a tee shirt. "Hakuna Matata," it read. That's "No Problem" in Swahili.

Sitting down at lunch with the college faculty, a department head leaned over to inquire, "This Michael Jackson. Is he normal?"

Sometimes I felt deeply moved by the spirit I thought I saw. There was a massive parade of bands from all over the world at an international festival in Geneva: a municipal band from Sweden, a folk group of Austrian peasants, a reed-and-drum corps of turbaned Arabs. Hundreds of spectators from all over the world photographed and applauded every band. I found myself in tears at the sight of it.

After the parade, I sat down at an outdoor cafe and struck up a conversation with the Swiss waitress. It turned out she was about to join her American boyfriend in San Francisco. They'd met as students at the University of California.

I visited with a couple of young Japanese teachers at the next table, on a whirlwind tour of Europe. They ticked off several countries where they'd been, then got stuck remembering Spain. "Where was that other place we stayed out late?" one asked the other. "You know, with the amigos!"

In England, we rode on the train with a young woman who'd spent her first years in Ireland. She had strong views of life in various sectors of the British Isles. Now she was on her way to join a merchandizing firm in Melbourne, marketing Australian furniture to wholesalers in southern California. She'd been there with her British business partners before, and she loved the excitement of Australia. "It's a new world now," she beamed. "You get to choose your home."

4 · *Moving Spirits*

Sometimes the spirit of change seemed almost boundless. I'd noticed signs of it back in Colorado. There were "New Age" business organizations for idealists who had grown up in the 1960s. They put on management conferences with as many workshops on Transcendental Meditation as on cost accounting.

Colorado's resort centers flowered with New Age global celebrations. John Naisbitt opened a conference center in the mountain town of Telluride, Colorado. He sponsored symposia with Russian intellectuals on "glasnost" and "perestroika."

Singer John Denver held conferences on world peace and environmental issues. One of them featured a talk by Ted Turner, the cable television magnate who had paid his dues when it came to global vision.

Several years ago, Turner invested $20 million in a "Goodwill Games" sports promotion in Moscow. The games were a financial disaster; Turner lost all his money. But many observers felt that the relationships he formed with Soviet broadcasters helped bring Ronald Reagan and Mikhail Gorbachev together, paving the way to détente.

I'd found another, unexpected facet of the new spirit in New Mexico, while gathering material for a newspaper article on economic development. New Mexico is a distinctive state – one of the poorest parts of the United States. Many Americans (whose ignorance of geography is legendary) don't even know it's part of their country.

Los Alamos is an anomaly in New Mexico. Birthplace of the

nuclear age, the city sits isolated on a narrow mesa of volcanic rock, surrounded by forested mountains. The main road twists up the mesa to a viewpoint at the east edge of town. From there, one can peer down at Espanola, the nearest town, fifteen miles away. From a height of 2000 feet, the view is surreal.

Residents of Los Alamos understand how removed they are from the rest of the state. Almost everyone works for the National Laboratory, where 1500 of the 8000 employees (ten per cent of the town) are PhDs. The laboratory was built on the grounds of a boarding school confiscated by the government during World War II. For two years its existence was kept secret, till the first atomic bomb fell on Hiroshima. Then New Mexicans learned of J. Robert Oppenheimer and other leading scientists living in their midst.

Employees of the laboratory are well aware of their economic distance from the rest of the state. In several nearby counties, populated by Indians and Hispanics, unemployment is over thirty-five per cent. They know that their high-paying jobs at the laboratory are almost entirely dependent on federal funds. Many of them remember that several times during post-war years the laboratory was almost shut down. And everyone in town recognizes that much of the recent government funding is tied to ex-President Reagan's fanciful Strategic Defense Initiative: the politically vulnerable Star Wars.

I was referred to officials at the Los Alamos Lab by state economic development officials in Santa Fe, the capital of New Mexico. They felt there was some interesting innovation going on there. I was astonished at what I found.

Civic leaders have been concerned about the future of the Los Alamos Laboratory for several years. There has been almost no new hiring, and some 300 houses – a record number – stand unsold. Some residents believe it's time to look for other sources of jobs, such as tourism. (The city is located at the center of eight Indian pueblos.) One resident seriously suggested marketing tours of the atom bomb laboratories to the Japanese, on the fiftieth anniversary of the attacks on Hiroshima and Nagasaki. There was a certain desperation in the air.

But other level-headed leaders have begun to convert part of the laboratory research to peacetime projects. Today, in fact, only fifty per cent of the lab's activity is devoted to nuclear weapons; twenty-five per cent is not defense-related at all. The laboratory has hired a physicist with an MBA from Massachusetts' high-tech-industry corridor to help commercialize Los Alamos' research.

The nation's mounting budget problems have raised many questions about military funding. They have highlighted both the inefficiencies of weapons research and the numbers of military bases that seem to serve only as a source of local civilian employment. (Canadians compare the US defense industry to their own system of income distribution: simply sending money to needy parts of their country.)

There is a growing belief that military activities are an inefficient source of jobs. Colorado economist Richard Williams cites data from the US Bureau of Labor Statistics: "Only thirty-four cents of each dollar spent on the military go to jobs," he notes. "By contrast, eighty-five cents of each dollar spent on education or health go to jobs, fifty-one cents in trade, forty cents in government, and thirty-nine cents in heavy industry."

Today, several organizations across the nation slog away at the task of freeing more of the American economy from defense. More of them today are opposing the weapons industry on economic as well as moral grounds. "We have to get at the economic underpinnings of the arms race," says Michael Closson of California's Center for Economic Conversion. Modern warfare is wrong because we can no longer afford it.

Many observers believe that economic conversion is coming, whatever its cost and dislocations. Hugh DeWitt, a staff physicist at the Livermore Laboratory in California, senses a growing expectation among defense scientists that the United States and the Soviet Union will sign a nuclear test ban treaty sometime early in the 1990s.

DeWitt has been an active proponent of such a treaty throughout his thirty-one-year careet at Livermore. He sees strong potential for energy research at his own facility: laser fusion, isotope separation for new forms of nuclear energy, surface physics research for more efficient solar energy.

There were some intriguing questions simmering quietly in New Mexico. Would arms reduction finally be achieved not so much through political action or protest as in the hard realities of unbalanced federal budgets and the plain need of defense scientists to find other ways of making a living? From North America to Africa, one wondered whether similar forces were not quietly at work in both places. Was it possible that a new global wave of commerce could carve a way to economic conversion as well?

If I had to give a name to the spirit I saw, it would be something like "free enterprise." At first I resisted that term. It was a favorite theme of British Prime Minister Margaret Thatcher and her fellow Tories in North America, Ronald Reagan and Canadian Prime Minister Brian Mulroney. All of them reveled in slogans like Thatcher's "enterprise culture."

Something of a knee-jerk liberal, I'd always equated "free enterprise" with "capitalism" – the accumulation of wealth. Both seemed simply code words for the interests of the rich. But slowly I learned to distinguish between capitalism and free enterprise. The notion of enterprise began to take on new meaning.

It was evident all over the world, for one thing, that almost every plan to direct the economic efforts of other people was failing. East Africa was a case in point.

Each of the region's three nations – Uganda, Tanzania, and Kenya – had taken a different route to development after independence. The countries have many similarities in language and culture, so the effects of their different strategies were apparent.

Uganda had built on some of the worst traditions of British colonialism, forming a society deeply divided between an aristocratic group in the south and a lower-income class in the Islamic north. Milton Obote, a self-serving aristocrat, appointed Idi Amin, a northen Muslim, to head the military; most of the soldiers came from the north. The rest is history. Now one finds highly educated Ugandan refugees all over the world.

Tanzania, under the idealistic socialist Julius Nyerere, tried to plan an independent economy based on shared wealth. Today the nation boasts a strong national culture with high levels of literacy in Swahili, but the economy is frail. Nyerere has retired from the presidency to set policy as chairman of the national party. From that position he is moving Tanzania toward a free-market economy.

Kenya has followed that course all along. To be sure, the country is less than affluent and faces serious population pressures. Nairobi, the capital city, is growing at twelve per cent annually and the nation itself at half that rate. Nonetheless, Kenya's economy clearly is the most viable of any in East Africa. There's evidence of sound planning for the future, too. The latest strategies emphasize the development of local economies.

The Swahili phrase "jua kali" translates to English as "hot sun."

The term is applied to a large class of Kenyan craftsmen who spend their days working by the side of the road, without shade. The *jua kali* are a resilient, self-reliant lot. One sees them turning out all kinds of products, from keys to charcoal burners, and performing a variety of services, from repairing shoes to cutting hair.

The *jua kali* embody Kenya's economic vision for the future. The government has begun building shelters for some of them. Technical training schools such as Friends College, Kaimosi, are being asked to offer them accounting and secretarial services. They represent a national commitment to entrepreneurial, grassroots development.

Free enterprise is not a new concept in Kenya. One of my Kenyan friends, Simeon Shitemi, told me a story of his old mentor Jomo Kenyatta, Kenya's first President. Soon after Kenya achieved independence from Britain, in 1963, the new President received an official visit from the Yugoslavian Marshal Tito.

Tito was met at Nairobi airport by a throng of reporters. "Why is it that you, a Communist leader, are here visiting a capitalist like Jomo Kenyatta?" one of them asked. "Why aren't you down in Tanzania calling on Julius Nyerere, your socialist brother?"

The Yugoslav blinked and considered the question. "Well, to begin with, Kenyatta and I are both old men," Tito replied. "We've been friends a long time. We're both political veterans."

"But there's another reason, too. I believe that Jomo Kenyatta is establishing a stronger basis for socialism through Kenya's free market economy than Nyerere with all his idealistic plans. You see, for socialism to succeed, first you must have something to share."

One Sunday afternoon in Kaimosi I sat reading *In the Age of the Smart Machine*, a new book on computers by a Harvard professor, Shoshana Zuboff. I had a lot of time to read, for I was expecting a visit from a group of Kenyan leaders who were attending a funeral down the road. I had no idea how long a Kenyan tribal funeral lasted, or when my guests would arrive.

The funeral was for a prominent local figure, the paramount chief: head of all the local tribes. High officials from all over the country had come to participate. This particular chief was legendary. He'd died at the age of 107, a vigorous man to the end. Till recently, the chief was still procuring business and political appointments for members of his family. He himself had retired from the government payroll only recently, at 105!

As it happened, the funeral lasted all day, despite a continuous rain; sounds of thunder mingled with the sonorous rhythms of drums. I pondered Zuboff's commentary on American business and technology. Her analysis was remarkably astute – the use of computers for automation or information, the ways computers enhanced or diminished jobs. I began to outline a review of the book for the newspaper.

But the drums echoed though the forest, reverberating in the rain. Part of me couldn't stop paying attention to the elegant rhythms, and considering what that funeral meant. I was struck by the strength of a culture where one person maintained his position into a second century, and hundreds of others stood out all day in their finest dress to honor him in the rain. Some powerful spirits were alive here, among people whose values could receive and sustain them.

I remembered a phrase from the New Testament, and it set me ruminating. "Test the spirits," John said. That's always seemed good advice, even coming from a couple of millennia ago. It's clear that Paul and Jesus lived in a time very different from our own – a world they found teeming with spirits both harmful and healthful, good and bad. These were powerful, demonic spirits. They could invade a human life and undo it.

The Gerasene demoniac whom Jesus met living out in a cemetery was a worst-case scenario. He was completely overcome by foreign spirits. "My name is Legion," he said, "for we are many." Jesus healed him, somehow helping him to integrate all his conflicting energies. But Jesus himself struggled with all kinds of demonic urges out in the wilderness. No one was immune to the spirits.

When they felt themselves in union with God's spirit, in fellowship with one another, people of biblical faith found strength against the demonic. They shared an empowering spirit. But they never felt invulnerable to other kinds of spirits – to overwhelming invasions of sorrow or wonder, fear or joy.

Sometimes I regret that we've lost so much of that sense of vulnerability today. There was a certain zest to the henotheism of biblical times: the need to seek one's own God without denying the existence of others. It was the abundance of all those other spirits that gave substance to one's own commitment. What if you chose the wrong God?

"Test the spirits," John said. He didn't suggest, like a monotheist, that we should deny them. Our culture mostly does. Today we seem to concentrate on studying life for a single explanatory cause. Ours is a worldly faith in the power of human reason to reduce the abundant mystery of life to a level where we can control it. It's a denuded, secular monotheism.

That may explain why I'd showed up in Kenya lugging a couple of heavy volumes on the changing American economy. Part modern-day, secular monotheist that I am, I was still seeking a thesis that would make sense of the transitions taking place back at home.

But I was beginning to tire of the theories of social analysts, and the bumper-sticker catchphrases used to promote their single-sided views: Megatrends, The Post-Industrial Age, The Age of the Smart Machine. No one theory seemed to grasp these times.

I thought of Paul again: "The letter kills, but the spirit gives life." Maybe he was right. Perhaps the best way to address all the changes of this churning world was simply to open oneself to the many living spirits one met there. That didn't negate intellectual analysis. There still was a need to name and distinguish the spirits one found. But the purpose of testing the spirits was not to ensconce them in concepts. It was learning to live among them, in the midst of the world, and listening for the rhythms of life.

The drums beat for the paramount chief.

5 · *Testing the Spirits*

It didn't take long to find spirits to be tested in Kenya. Beneath the bright vista of a common global culture, there were some powerful forces at work in world trade.

It was evident that computers were being marketed all across Africa. I picked up a high-tech magazine in Nairobi and read about IBM's new strategic marketing plan for Uganda. The story seemed preposterous. One of my Kenyan friends had been shot at, on a medical mission in Uganda a month before. He got caught in cross-fire between government troops and rebels out in the countryside.

Uganda was rife with destruction – littered with piles of skulls from two decades of civil war and reeling from a rampant epidemic of AIDS. The country didn't seem primed for a technological revolution. But evidently multinational interests had a timetable of their own. Here was IBM's agenda for Uganda.

Many Kenyans were excited by the new information technology. I talked with a banker from Nakuru, a small city on the shore of a lake with a great pink flock of wild flamingoes. He was in Nairobi attending a training course on a new automated financial records system for his bank.

It seemed that some marketing officer had thought up a novel promotion that had multiplied their sales in a matter of months. Depositors were offered a free insurance policy for death or disability resulting from highway accidents. This was an inspired scheme, for auto accidents were a daily fact of life and death in Kenya. With a population of only 20 million, the country had the sixth-highest number of traffic fatalities in the world.

The problem was implementing the plan. Currently, each transaction in the bank had to be processed manually by three employees. With the new promotion, suddenly the Nakuru branch had 25,000 depositors. His staff was working evenings and weekends, but still they could not keep up. Computers were the answer.

Government agencies were automating their operations, too. For the first time, Kenya's legislative assembly was receiving budgetary information on schedule, while they were still in session.

In Kaimosi, I found the Friends College faculty eager to add computers to their curriculum. As we met to discuss long-range plans for the college, the subject came up again and again. The students were receiving good instruction in secretarial skills and accounting. But they were graduating into automated office environments having never laid hands on a computer.

The school needed updated equipment, not only for the students but for the local community was well. More and more, Friends College was being asked to offer small business services to local entrepreneurs such as the *jua kali*. Computers could support spreadsheet accounting and word processing, and provide automated assistance filling out government forms.

I knew of a small foundation in Colorado that probably could provide computers. Daryl Maus, a high-tech inventor in Boulder, had conceived of the Global Technology Foundation one day when he was throwing out an old computer. "Surely somebody could use this," he thought. "Maybe someone in the Third World."

Several friends had taken to his idea. They began contacting businesses that were upgrading their computer systems, asking for the used equipment and distributing it to non-profit agencies in developing countries. This seemed a perfect program for Kaimosi.

Still I found myself harboring questions about computers in Kenya. Are you sure you want to get involved in this? Based on my experiences back in the States, I couldn't get past the question of employment.

The American labor market is a maelstrom. Each year in the United States, one-third of our future jobs are in process of formation, one-third of our technical skills turn obsolescent, and one-third of our workers leave their jobs.

The process is accelerating. Twenty-five years ago, the average time an American worker held a job was 4.6 years; today it's 3.6 years. That's almost as short as a career in the violent National Football League. Those players last an average of 3.5 years.

There is nothing new, of course, about job change. Occupational roles have come and gone throughout history. There is a typical example in Thomas Hardy's novel, *The Return of the Native*: an affectionate, unhurried view of rural England in the mid-nineteenth century. The setting is evening, out on the barren heath. An old man is walking slowly down the road. He is gazing at an object in the distance.

> When he drew nearer he perceived it to be a spring van, ordinary in shape but singular in colour, this being a lurid red. The driver walked beside it; and, like his van, he was completely red. One dye of that tincture covered his clothes, the cap upon his head, his boots, his face, and his hands. He was not temporarily overlaid with the colour; it permeated him.
>
> The old man knew the meaning of this. The traveller with the cart was a reddleman – a person whose vocation it was to supply farmers with redding for their sheep. He was one of a class rapidly becoming extinct in Wessex, filling at present in the rural world the place which, during the last century, the dodo occupied in the world of animals. He is a curious, interesting, and nearly perished link between obsolete forms of life and those which generally prevail.

Sometimes in a class or an informal talk, I've asked my audience to listen to that vignette with their eyes closed. There's a cadence about it that summons up the pastoral world Hardy remembered and savored, as he wrote near the turn of the century. That had been a quiet age, where change still bore a human form and its pace seemed somewhat measured.

By Hardy's time, of course, that kind of world was vanishing fast. The Industrial Revolution could be felt everywhere in England as the new technology picked up steam. People were no longer phasing out of obsolescent jobs, like the last, lingering days of the dodo bird. They were thrown out of work abruptly, forced to give up homesteads in the countryside for unimaginable lives in the cities of the new industrial age.

Today that kind of transition is rampant. And it's not just the breakneck speed of the process that is so devastating. Mostly it's the sense that it's running out of control.

Not long ago a social scientist in Atlanta, Georgia, published a fascinating study of stress and self-control in the field of auto racing. Professional drivers were tested for stress in two settings: racing 200 miles an hour around the track, then sitting idle while their cars were being serviced during pit stops. It turned out the drivers' stress levels were much higher when they had to depend on the actions of others, in the pit stops.

It's clear today that we know much more about the effects of changing employment in a churning economy than about the causes of it. And it's evident that we understand even less what to do.

We know that technology always changes jobs, in ways that affect the whole lives of workers. Research has shown that as unemployment rises, homicide, suicide, and illness increase at a higher rate. My impression from many years experience counseling unemployed people is that these symptoms of stress are linked to the loss of autonomy that people experience when they're out of work.

This sense of powerlessness seems widespread today within organized labor. I was in England when the electrical union walked out of the annual seaside labor conference. The union, Britain's second largest and most white-collared labor body, had signed a vertical pact with a large employer. In the ensuing rancor at the labor congress, the electricians were essentially forced out.

Yet, according to Jurek Martin, foreign editor of the London *Financial Times*, agreements of that kind are on the upswing. They're already common in Japan. The reason may be that in a field as full of fluctuation as electronics, it's difficult to organize workers any other way. How do you maintain a union of people whose required skills and job titles change on average every three years?

Few professional people I spoke with in Britain grieved much over the labor strife; unions are no more popular in England than in the United States. Today more Americans own their own businesses than belong to labor unions. Some believe that's another reason to celebrate the *Zeitgeist* of free enterprise.

But it's hard not to worry about the welfare of workers in a country such as Britain that has no minimum wage law, or in the US, where the minimum wage is so low that masses of employed people have no homes. Rapid technological change weakens the position of employees in the work place. Sometimes it costs them their jobs.

I met Beth as a bed-and-breakfast hostess in western Canada. I stayed at her place in Calgary. Beth had served as executive secretary to the chief financial officer of an oil company for twenty years. She was recognized as a good office manager with strong secretarial skills. In business school she had won a prize in shorthand, and she especially enjoyed taking dictation.

Five years ago, Beth's company introduced a new computer system. The system was expensive, and the firm encouraged all its executives to complete a training program in text-editing so that they could draft their own correspondence.

Beth was called in less frequently to take dictation. She found herself resenting the new computer system and slow to learn it. The company sent her to three different courses in word-processing and spreadsheet accounting before concluding that she was just not cut out for the new technology.

Her boss was directed to hire a new secretary with good computer skills. At fifty-five, Beth decided to take early retirement rather than accept a humilating demotion. Now she supports herself taking in bed-and-breakfast guests. She's solvent but sometimes misses her friends at work. A substantial part of her life is gone.

I thought of Beth in Kenya, where they go to great lengths to create jobs, often at the expense of efficiency. A journey through customs at Nairobi's Kenyatta Airport was a nightmare of bureaucracy. One spent an hour (at best, if lucky) completing the same transaction with several different officials. Exchanging currency at a bank was even worse. But each step in every convoluted process provided some clerk with a job.

I bought a couple of items at the University of Nairobi bookstore and dealt with three different clerks. One totaled my purchase and wrote the chit. The second wrapped up my books. The third clerk checked the calculation of the first and took payment.

Walking back to the hotel, I passed an auto accident on Uhuru Drive. It was a minor accident involving a dented fender. But ten policemen were investigating it. Redundancy engendered employment.

When my Kenyan friend Simeon Shitemi visited Denver, we stopped by my bank. I took out my Automated Teller Machine card to use the cash machine in the lobby. Simeon hadn't seen that new technology. Then we went inside so he could cash a travelers check. I pointed to the tellers' windows, half of which were closed. The tellers had been supplanted by ATM cards.

I remembered five Kenyans conducting a manual speed check on the road from the airport (the kind of operation one American policeman would run with a radar gun). And the dozens of construction workers, raising and lowering buckets of cement at a construction site. An industrialized country would have a machine for that.

"Do you really want this technology in Kenya?" I wondered. What about all those young people wandering the streets, looking for work in Nairobi? Without doubt, that airport customs operation is a hassle, but it represents jobs.

I posed my question to Sarah Lukalo, a Kenyan educator who'd experienced life in both North America and Africa. She'd studied at Harvard. Like a good teacher, Sarah answered with a question in return. "Can we ever solve one problem by adding another?" she asked. "Is inefficiency a solution to unemployment?"

Now and then, the analyst in me wished there were time to organize a seminar in Nairobi and consider some basic questions. Not just about computer technology and employment, but the whole global economic scene. Where is this new economy going? What forces are driving it so fast? And do you Africans really want to join it?

The questions, of course, were actually about life in America. Most of our own economists had yet to consider them. Harvard professor Robert Reich, one-time economic adviser to Presidential candidate Gary Hart, had written an insightful book on America's position in the new global economy: *The Next American Frontier*. But the book was full of unexamined assumptions about the goals of economic activity. Like many Western economists, Reich seems to view life as a contest of speed.

> The only way industrialized nations can increase their citizens' standards of living in the future is to concentrate on the high-value niches within (traditional) industries and to *seize and keep world leadership in new industries based on advanced and emerging technologies* ... Japan understands this future. So, to a lesser extent, do West Germany and France. They know that *economic success will depend upon the speed* and appropriateness of their shift in production ... Governments and business in *these nations therefore are racing* to gain sophistication in these new sectors ... (my italics).

The same notion pervades most literature on economic development in the US. It seems that the paradigm for life is a race. That assumption has been questioned plenty of times in the past. Gandhi observed: "There is more to life than increasing its speed." "Anything worth doing is worth doing slowly," Mae West is thought to have said.

Today we in the "developed" nations seem to be losing the capacity to ask those kinds of questions. Yet even one or two hands-on encounters with fast-changing technology can call them to mind.

Several years ago I enrolled in an intensive computer software class down at the Denver Technological Center. I was managing the development of a new computer system at work. The system was being programmed in dBase III, and it seemed that learning something about that software would help me communicate more effectively with the programmer.

In the two weeks between the time I enrolled in the class and the day it began, the software company came out with an updated version of the program: dBase III PLUS. Evidently the change occurred almost overnight; no one told the instructor.

The first morning, we twenty students booted up the new software in our individual computers. Then we began working through the old manual of instructions under the direction of our teacher.

All went well till we arrived at one particular command from the old manual, about an hour into the class. The new software did not cotton on to that old command. One by one, as each student performed the operation, his computer shut down.

The instructor turned from one person to the next, trying to correct our errors. Soon he was racing among us. Then suddenly he stopped in the aisle and stood there, looking befuddled. He began to see his predicament full-scale, and his face turned white. Here he had a roomful of students, tuition-paid. Yesterday, he'd been competent to teach us. But the knowledge he'd brought to class had turned obsolescent overnight.

Ashton-Tate, the California firm that developed dBase III, is no different from any other software house. They revise their product every year; by now they're marketing dBase V. The reason for the revisions is largely economic. Computers, unlike heavy machinery such as automobiles, hardly ever wear out. With normal use, the average home computer will last a lifetime.

Software represents a vital "after market" for the data processing industry. Consumers must be convinced periodically that the product they own is obsolescent. In an information industry, that kind of marketing regularly turns skills obsolescent as well. That's one of the reasons we "developed" countries suffer from rampant change.

The other reason has to do with international politics. Two of the economic competitors cited by Reich – Japan and West Germany – were adversaries of a different sort not so very long ago in World War II. We all can be grateful that the horrors of that kind of conflict may be past. Now competition is economic. As Naisbitt points out, in an integrated global economy it's unlikely America would even consider another nuclear attack on the Japanese.

But there's a disquieting, combative spirit in today's economic race. Americans rousing from narcosis are increasingly aware of it. They recognize that Japan is acquiring US assets at an unprecedented rate. Here in Colorado, a second major ski resort has been purchased by a Japanese corporation. One of our private colleges was just sold to a university in Japan. Now it's an overseas study center for their students.

Some analysts are encouraged by this development. Joel Kotkin, an editor of *Inc. Magazine*, has a best-selling book, *The Third Century*, on welcoming Japanese trade and investment. Japanese investors are a good omen for America, according to Kotkin. After all, if the Orientals lacked confidence in our economy, would they be buying it up?

Others accuse Americans of racism. British and Canadian investment in America is many times that of the Japanese; why doesn't it cause the same concern?

And then, of course, there are the prophets of decline. So what if America's economic contest with the rest of the world becomes a losing race? It's time to even up the global score. Here we go, down the same road as Britain.

Still, it seems there are larger questions at stake than those. For me, they're based on the premise that economic competition has value. I've listened to the complaints of too many visitors from Marxist countries not to recognize the benefits of individual incentive. I believe in free enterprise through competition. But that's not what we have today.

Our contest in global trade is unequal, for one thing. The US is hamstrung by lingering fears of Japanese and German expansionism. It's hard not to ask what the US economic position would be were we not underwriting the defense budgets of Japan and West Germany –

our two chief economic competitors. A trading race in which one of the participants ties up much of its scientific talent in farcical projects such as Minute Man Missiles and Star Wars hardly seems a contest at all.

That's a good part of the reason we're circling the track at such a frantic pace: we don't trust one another. At a deep, unspoken level, the pain and fear of old wars continue to motivate this race.

There's a spiritual problem beneath the gloss of today's new global economy. In a world that needs collaborative solutions to common problems, our "developed" nations are caught up in transmogrified combat. It's not the race itself that's wrong, but the way we're all running it. We're going too fast to consider common goals.

There were 300 Japanese in Kenya. One was a distinguished, middle-aged man who appeared to be on a long-term trade mission in Nairobi. Each evening he ate and drank alone at the United Kenya Club.

One hundred of the others were members of the Japanese Overseas Corporation of Volunteers, a Japanese Peace Corps. Seigo was a JOCV volunteer teaching in the food technology department at Friends College. He was apparently well-trained in food-processing but had arrived in Kaimosi with no knowledge of either English or Swahili.

That piqued my curiosity about the JOCV. Seigo was a warm, collegial fellow. But I wondered who had thought to send him to Africa so ill-prepared. Were the volunteers basically humanitarians? Or were they some kind of economic good will ambassadors, breaking ground for the commercial interests of Japan?

When I'd visited Daryl Maus's lab in Boulder, Colorado, to talk about the Global Technology Foundation computers, he and his staff were rushing off for a game of laser tag. It seems there's a big converted warehouse in Boulder where you pay to chase other people around the darkened room, firing harmless laser rays at targets that pop up around the walls, and at one another.

Daryl works in a computer lab that glows with screens of multi-colored designs in three-dimensional graphics. These are inventions for aerospace and biotechnology. His walls are lined with pictures and quotations of Einstein. He's the kind of intellectual who seems to belong in the next century.

But Daryl is a thoughtful, caring person. I once asked him why he'd devoted so much effort to a foundation that still could not afford a full-time staff member or an office. It's always hard to raise money for projects overseas.

"This is grassroots philanthropy, all right," he grinned. "But it's a way for us to act globally with something that's of interest to us."

He and his associates were thinking of branching out into telecommunications technology. It turns out there's just as much usable telephone equipment available as computers. The People's Republic of China sent a delegation to Colorado to look over some available equipment. They were expected to pay enough for the equipment to fund an office for the foundation.

The Chinese checked out the equipment: it worked well. It's the same technology found in forty per cent of the US telecommunications system. The equipment could contribute to the development of China, where half the nation has no telephone service.

But the effort failed. "Why?", I asked Daryl.

"They found out it was less than state-of-the-art," he sighed. "'We only want the latest thing,' the Chinese said."

I thought about communications in the part of Kenya where the computers were going. In my visits to Kenyan homes, I'd seen all sorts of telecommunications technology. There was short-wave radio for credible, long-distance news. Then there was the ineffective telephone system, always breaking down, and an operator who compensated for poor connections by screaming directions to her callers like a military drill sergeant.

The most efficient method of telecommunication seemed to be drumming. The drums sounded all hours of the day and night. After a while, one learned to listen for the cadence. A slow drumming beat announced a funeral. Up-tempo drums signified a happy event such as a wedding, or a film that night in the open market. One could even follow the scores of soccer games by drum. Every team had a distinctive beat, and the officials would play that riff each time they scored.

I had a feeling Daryl Maus would get along well in Kenya. My friends there would like him, just as they'd accepted Seigo. The Friends College faculty had helped the young Japanese teach food preparation by physical demonstration till he learned a bit of Swahili and English. He'd made some good friends in Africa. The last time I saw him he was riding on a motorcycle with Benson, a young Kenyan teacher who was opening a bookstore next to the open market.

Seigo was about to leave on a long motorcycle trip through northern Africa with some other JOCV volunteers. The Japanese had heard impressive stories about Egyptian women, and they were off to investigate. My American associates would appreciate that spirit, too.

Colorado business owners would understand why Friends College staff are interested in computers, to provide support services for entrepreneurs such as Benson and the *jua kali*. Coloradans could understand the importance of grassroots economic development in a place like Kaimosi. They're struggling to rebuild an economy themselves.

Sometimes I imagine that computers could be tendrils of communication – building global, human ties. It's the kind of vision I believe E.F. Schumacher would share if he were alive today. Wouldn't he see the Global Technology Foundation as an expression of appropriate technology: economics as if people mattered? It seems to me they're following in his spirit.

And sometimes my daydreams run further. I envision all the people who have worked on the project bringing computers to Kaimosi. Maybe we'd be meeting for an evening meal. Or sharing our various technologies. We'd need some time to learn new skills – computer graphics, foreign languages, maybe laser tag and the meaning of the drums. But knowing those people as I do, I'm sure we'd enjoy that exchange. We would all learn from one another. I'm convinced we'd get along. If only we could call a halt to this infernal race.

6 · *Third World Questions*

There were many quiet evenings in Kenya when I did have dinner with friends and we talked late into the night. Sometimes we watched television from the Voice of Kenya. That is, we actually watched it. Kenyans paid attention to television, much as Americans used to in the early 1950s before the numbers of channels proliferated and the novelty of the medium wore off.

In Kenya, a television sat covered with a lace doily. The unveiling of the set was something of an occasion. Guests sat quietly through one- and two-hour programs. No one talked over the television, unlike in the US, where TVs function mostly as background noise.

Since there was only one channel in the country, there was little controversy over what to watch. And one could always count on finding others to discuss the program one saw the following day. There was something unifying about television in Kenya.

I enjoyed the African sports programs – the famed Kenyan distance runners who won five gold medals in the 1988 Olympics, field hockey and soccer from the Pan African games. One of the soccer teams had a giant mascot in a panther costume who led cheers and danced to drumming in the stands.

There were American sports programs as well – mostly highlights from the National Basketball Association. Deep in the heart of Africa, we spoke of Magic Johnson and the impending retirement of Kareem Abdul Jabar.

It seemed that basketball was part of the new global culture. Kenyans played a variant of it called "netball," where players did everything but dribble. It was a good adaptation for outdoor courts where there was no level playing surface.

Africans were beginning to join Europeans as players in the NBA. Today the best center in the world is Nigerian. The tallest player is Manute Bol – a spindly seven-foot-five-inch Dinka tribesman from the Sudan. When Bol entered the league three years ago, he reminded one less of an athlete than a tree. But he's made steady improvement and now is one of the most respected shot-blockers in the NBA.

Recently a newspaper in Dallas, Texas, sent a reporter over to the Sudan to report on the civil war. While there, the reporter decided to look up Manute Bol's family. He was curious to learn how they regarded their tribesman's new athletic career.

It turns out the global culture still has gaps. Bol's relatives had no idea what he was doing in America. They did have some bad news for him. His uncle, Nquol Bol, told the reporter: "If Manute is still alive, tell him his wife has married another man and most of his cattle were stolen by the Arab militia."

Albion George, the deputy chief of Bol's tribe, said: "If he has no cows and wants to marry an American wife, we can get the cows together for him. Just let us know how many cows the woman's family demands."

"If he needs any help, we are still here," his uncle assured him.

There is a warm side to African tribal life that isn't covered much in the Western press. Most of it appears as tragic conflict. Some of the conflicts between tribes certainly are horrendous. They generally involve groups such as Bol's Dinkas who were dumped with rival tribes into "nations" by the nineteenth century colonizers from Europe.

African tribes had bloody conflicts even before the Europeans divided up their continent. Isolated by dense jungle and scorching desert, they held one another in suspicion. African tribes fought bloody wars and readily sold captives into slavery.

Today national boundaries persist long after the Europeans who drew them up have left, and the rancor among African tribes is even worse. Tribal rivalries take many forms – from outright genocide in places like Burundi and the Sudan, to political repression by dictators who seize and maintain power on the promise of *Pax Romana*.

One Zambia! One nation.
One nation! One party.
One party! One leader.

To citizens of a strife-torn country such as Uganda, the blandishments of a strong ruler like Zambia's Kenneth Kaunda may seem an attractive alternative to chronic civil war.

Western powers have produced some sophisticated analysts of African problems. Mostly they're doomsayers. Robert McNamara of the World Bank had this to say to a group of agricultural economists last year in Washington:

> The harsh truth is that sub-Saharan Africa today faces a crisis of unprecedented proportions. The physical environment is deteriorating. Per capita production of food grains is falling. Population growth rates are the highest in the world and rising. National economics are in disarray. And international assistance in real terms is moving sharply downward.

International support will not be easy to mobilize, McNamara warned, if concerns persist in industrial nations over a number of serious problems: "pervasiveness of corruption ... use of scarce resources to build defense establishments and luxury projects ... harsh treatment of regional groups and repression of internal dissent."

McNamara's pronouncement is a sobering reminder of some genuinely serious problems that receive too little attention in the West. He's one of too few Western leaders who pay attention to developments in the Dark Continent.

But he misses quite a lot as well. That's not surprising. Robert McNamara is a notoriously myopic technocrat, still remembered in America for his misperceptions of Vietnam. Here, he obscures the human meaning of Africa's "regional groups" – the soft side of tribalism. Tribes offer Africans a place to feel at home in the world, in a culture to call one's own.

I myself am no expert on Africa. I've only read a bit about the continent and been there twice. But I'm sensitive enough to my surroundings to appreciate alternative values. Now and then in Kenya I found myself in the presence of some different perspectives I couldn't ignore.

One night there was a dinner party at Moses Simani's house. Moses is a big, impressive man who spent most of his career in the foreign service. He headed Kenya's embassy in Paris and served for a number of years in Ottawa, Ontario. As it happens, that's where my father grew up.

I was looking forward to spending the evening with Moses' family and friends, and hearing his impressions of Ottawa. He came by to pick me up in a heavy rain. The first thing he said was, "Did you see where Ernest went?"

Ernest Gituma was an instructor at Friends College. After work, he'd walked with me through the downpour and headed off up the road to hitch a ride home in the rain. Ernest's wife and children were visiting from Nairobi where she ran a small business.

I hadn't known Ernest was invited to the Simanis, and I wasn't sure where he lived. But Moses was intent on finding him. For almost an hour, we drove slowly along the highway. Moses would pull over to a cluster of houses, a filling station, or a tavern and go out in search of Ernest. Each time, he'd come back soaking wet. On something like the tenth stop, he found him.

Naturally, the dinner was late. However, that was not unusual in Kenya. Some industries such as the airlines kept to schedules, but the most part, time was approximate and organic, melded with the day. "I'll come by to see you in the late morning." Or "mid-afternoon," or "sometime after supper." Kenyans seemed to subordinate time to personal relations. Finding Ernest and inviting his wife to dinner meant more than serving the first course on schedule.

Kenyans who'd lived overseas were keenly aware of different cultural values. Moses regaled us all one night with impressions of North America. He described family life in eastern Canada. There was the family gathering on Boxing Day at Christmas in Ottawa when teenage cousins were introduced as strangers. It was hard for the other Kenyans to conceive of cousins who hadn't met. He tried to explain how lawyers were engaged to draw up wills – a totally foreign concept to the others.

I especially remember his description of driving on the freeways of Canada. "You move along incredibly fast," he explained. "One hundred kilometers an hour down a four-lane highway! If you want to leave the freeway, you must find your way over to the side miles ahead of the exit. Miss the exit and you are lost! And all the time, of course, everyone is speeding by you. One hundred kilometers an hour!"

Bernadette Canute, Principal of the College, was listening quietly with a puzzled frown. She is a bright, inquisitive person who has never been outside East Africa. Bernadette looked up at Moses, shaking her head. "What's the hurry?" she asked him.

My impressions of Africa are only that. They're partly reflections, like Moses' stories, of my own state of mind. But I valued the Africans' perspective on the culture I'd come from. They still could ask good questions. What's the hurry, indeed?

Some of the questions put to me were challenging. "Now then, what about Michael Jackson? Who does he think he is? Does he know?" a Ugandan woman asked me on an airplane, late one night.

I'd become accustomed to Michael Jackson questions from curious Africans, but I wasn't good at answering them. I'd mumble half-baked analyses of the young American rock star. There was Michael Jackson's admiration for Diana Ross of the Supremes (which presumably could account for having himself made over to look like her). Or the quality of life in Gary, Indiana (which could induce anyone who grew up there to do almost anything to escape it).

As a kind of last-ditch, immaterial defense, I'd mention his humanitarianism: Michael Jackson gave away much of his earnings. He cared about people, appearing in music videos with youngsters from all over the world.

That's when I stumbled upon another explanation. I'd been reading an article about new global merchandizing strategies. It seems that advanced communication and transportation technology is revolutionizing the way popular products are sold. More and more these days, fashionable products such as tape players and sports apparel are manufactured for "niche markets" of consumers based not on nationality but age.

That's because twenty-five-year-old consumers from Argentina or France now have more similar tastes than either has to, say, forty-year-olds in their own countries. International marketing specialists are learning to connect with these vast, world-wide consumer groups – to shape as well as meet their expectations.

Suddenly, it seemed I understood Michael Jackson. What if his plastic surgery were calculated to create the very kind of apparition he now conveyed: an aracial, asexual, international androgyne? A person with no particular race or sex? A universal media figure for a global, pre-teen market?

It was one of those theories that always sounds best at three o'clock in the morning. But given what one saw in merchandizing, it made sense. World markets were becoming homogenized.

So were local cultures. Jurek Martin of the *Financial Times* of London participated in an international conference last year in Colorado. He took part in a panel entitled, "True Brit: There'll Always Be an England."

Not so, said Martin. Just about the only local culture left in England is the thatched-roof cottages, pubs, and country lanes set out for tourists. "All of Britain is reduced to a theme park," he lamented.

Martin himself is a pure global citizen. His office at the *Financial Times*, across the street from St Paul's Cathedral, is festooned with objects from assignments all over the world: Japanese pottery, a picture of the 1969 New York Mets. The morning I met him in London, Martin stumbled in from a late night watching the French Open tennis tournament on his video cassette recorder. He'd missed seeing it live, flying in from New York. The day after tomorrow, he'd be off for Africa.

I knew globe-trotting Africans who were just as cosmopolitan as Martin. People like Moses Simani, who had a picture of himself with the Pope, were at home anywhere in the world. But the Africans took a different approach to residence. Ask a Kenyan "Where are you from?" and he'll be likely to name a tribal village. Then he'll add, "I stay in Nairobi," or wherever.

African culture cost something, to be sure. It didn't just happen. City-dwellers spent hours traveling back to ancestral villages on weekends to keep in touch with relatives at home. That's one reason for all the traffic fatalities.

On the outskirts of Nairobi there is a daily program of tribal music and dance at a place called the Bomas. It's the kind of performance – drums and flutes and grass skirts – apparently contrived for tourists. But each time I've seen the show, the audience has been mostly African. The Bomas are a tie to tradition in an electronic age, an entertaining way of staying grounded.

Most Africans seem to keep track of their origins in a way that most Americans do not. We are polyglot products of a common melting pot. That's a trait many Americans are proud of. It may be that our ethnic diversity has broadened our base of shared experience and contributed to our creativity as a nation. But it's also a factor in the American sense of sometimes feeling quite lost and adrift and alone.

"How many tribes do you have?" African children asked me. Or, even more baffling, "What tribe are you from?" Where do you belong? It had been to find answers to those basic questions that I'd set out in search of my father's origins in Canada.

7 · *Elusive Tribes*

If you have to go looking for your roots, Canada is a fascinating place to do it. As one soon discovers, the whole country has an identity problem of its own. Scrutinizing Canada's fragile culture and determining whether and where to keep that culture alive is perhaps the nation's oldest tradition.

The country's first European settlers were trappers and prospectors employed by private firms such as the Hudson's Bay Company. After the American War of Independence, British Loyalists flocked into Canada to join them and another large contingent of French-speaking farmers. These were the colonists France had abandoned when they lost their North American war with England.

That Canada was a nation at all was an accident of British foreign policy. In the nineteenth century, England found itself with a vast, North American territory flush against a poorly defined border with the young, expansionist United States. The Pacific Coast Gold Rush had stoked America's lust for new lands. Britain decided that North America could do with a bit more structure, and Canada was born.

As a nation with strong ethnic, political, and cultural ties to a contiguous country ten times its size, Canada has faced many of the same challenges as Scotland with England. I've been struck by some of the similar, subtle ways England and the United States discount their neighbors to the north. Try following news from Scotland or Canada, or using their currency south of the border.

The Scots, nonetheless, have a clear sense of heritage. I'll never forget a concert by the Corries in Portree on the Isle of Skye. The crowd thronged the town hall to hear the popular singing group, some of them decked out in kilts. They sang along verse after verse of Scottish songs, one of them the national anthem. After the concert someone brought a bagpipe and accordion down to a bar, and the singing carried on late into the night.

Canada has no obvious traditions like that. An apparent appendage to the United States, the nation has been described as "geographically ridiculous and politically impossible." That's why cultivating Canadian culture has proved so difficult.

In the nineteenth century America's interest in western Canada remained strong, even after Canadian independence. There was some possibility that British Columbia might secede to the US. That's when Canada built her intercontinental railway to link both coasts together.

When the age of electronic communication arrived in the early twentieth century, and radio programs flooded north from America, Canadians sensed another more insidious danger. The nation could drown in imported popular culture unless it mobilized to create an entertainment vessel of its own. "It's the State, or the States," one official put it. That's when the Canadian Broadcasting Company was born.

Today, despite these precautions, ninety per cent of the music, literature and media programming in Canada originates in the United States. Canadians accept that common culture. But now and then, when the northern nation fears it may be absorbed by everything American, it invents new measures to safeguard some sort of national identity.

There's the subsidizing of local artists, for example. Canadians can apply for funding from a generous store of grants. Or there's the requirement that Canadian broadcasting media feature a certain percentage of local performers. Musicians such as Gordon Lightfoot or Joni Mitchell, who now have a world-wide following, first got their start because the CBC was required to offer them a hearing.

I found that's typical of Canada. There's a sense of commonweal up there that stands out in contrast to the *laissez-faire* ethic of the United States. Perhaps it comes from centuries of joining forces against an imperiling environment.

It's a spirit reflected in Canada's comprehensive health insurance, a program now being studied in the US, where thirty-seven million people have no health-care coverage. Even income is shared in

Canada. People in rugged, outlying parts of the country are subsidized to live there. "Regional equalization" is a long-standing Canadian tradition. Keeping the vast country occupied is seen as important to national defense.

There are drawbacks to this sort of socialism, to be sure. Some of the artists who receive subsidies, whose records are played on the CBC and whose novels show up in bookstores, are not gifted. They'd never survive on the open market.

In addition, conservative critics warn that subsidies may vitiate Canadians' incentive. The way things were going, free trade proponents argued, Canada could devolve into a "giant sheltered workshop" for the incompetent and otherwise unemployed. Canadians confront many of the same questions one hears today from advocates of the enterprise culture in Britain.

Is there a Canadian culture? That's a perennial question. Every fight to save Canadian culture seems to coincide with efforts to find it. Certainly there's something deeper there than socialist politics. A traveler who looks closely for the non-American elements in Canada is sure to find a vibrant, native spirit about the place.

Charitable fund-raising, for example, has a local flavor very much like the *harambee* self-help projects that pervade Kenya. In Canada, fund-raising gives rise to a continuous round of home-grown, gala events.

There's the 1988 Great Alberta Duck Race: 46,000 plastic ducks, each numbered and sold for a $5 donation to the Alberta Heart and Stroke Foundation. On Labour Day in Calgary the entire flock was dumped into the Bow River for a one-and-a-half-kilometer float to the finish line downstream. The contestant whose numbered duck arrived first won a car.

Or the paper-airplane-flying contest I saw during half-time of a football game in Vancouver. This event was to benefit the Easter Seal foundation for birth defects. Everyone received a fold-your-own paper airplane kit at the gate. During the intermission, a car was set out at mid-field. Then everyone let fly on signal, and the numbered plane landing closest to the car won it.

Football is a microcosm of popular culture in Canada. It's a source of tradition, for one thing, since North American football is essentially a Canadian invention. In 1874 a group of students from Montreal's McGill University traveled down to Cambridge, Massachusetts, for a rugby match with Harvard. The McGill students had been experimenting with a modification of the Rugby rules, using an oval ball and pre-established plays.

Harvard's players liked the game so well that they continued to develop it, too. North American football evolved along two, parallel lines as colleges in both countries adopted the game and professional leagues developed as well. Football is a tradition shared with Americans; it's typically Canadian in that way, too.

The first Canadian Football League game I saw, in August 1987, was an exercise in seeking Canada. The game was played on a balmy, late-summer day in Vancouver, British Columbia — a gorgeous city surrounded by ocean, mountains, and forests.

A crowd of 38,000 drifted into the domed stadium on the waterfront, dressed in tee shirts and shorts as though summoned from the beach. They filtered in slowly and perhaps reluctantly, for the temperature inside was 85 degrees and the stadium felt like a sauna. The BC Lions drew better crowds at night, but television commitments called for a day game to reach the major share of viewers three time zones to the east.

From the press box it was difficult to identify much of the scene as Canadian; the atmosphere seemed more like California. Some of the fans bounced a beach ball through the stands. A bevy of cheerleaders bounced to "La Bamba." Crazy George, a professional cheerleader from San Jose, California, exorted the crowd as he banged his drum.

Everyone stood respectfully for the national anthem, but I noted that the scoreboard lined out the words. The sense of national identity seemed frail.

Canadian football looked American as well, although some differences were apparent: the field was longer and wider, there were twelve players to a side, and the teams had three downs rather than four to gain ten yards. The game was swift-moving, faster than America's National Football League, with twenty seconds between plays and no time-outs till the last three minutes of each half. None that is except those for TV commercials, which were as frequent as in the States.

There was a certain nonchalance about the game. On a change of possession, players were still walking off field as the next series of downs began. The scoreboard briefly credited a touchdown to the wrong team. While an occasional fight broke out, it was common to see players help up others from the opposition.

Neither team scored a touchdown or field goal in the first quarter, yet Winnipeg led by a point. It seemed that a one-point rouge was awarded every time a ball landed unreturned in the end zone; the Blue Bombers' scored one for a missed field goal. This rule was utterly foreign to American football.

One noticed other differences, too. CFL football at first seemed to lack continuity; with only three downs to move the football and a longer field to cover, there were few sustained drives. The action, instead, was episodic, exploding from an apparently endless round of turnovers, and the scores seemed to come in bunches. Winnipeg fell apart near the end of the first half and gave up fourteen points on pass interceptions in the span of twenty seconds.

Winnipeg rallied in the second half for a touchdown and two field goals, and with thirty-six seconds left the score was 14–all. Now BC had the ball at mid-field and could run out the clock till overtime. But as the Lions lined up, the crowd stirred, sensing another possibility. The cheerleaders and music fell silent.

A low murmur rose in the stadium and grew to a roar as Lui Passaglia, the BC kicker and a Vancouver native, trotted onto the field. The crowd indeed knew what was coming; they were going to try a rouge! Passaglia got off a soaring punt that carried fifty-three yards and hung in the air four seconds before Ken Winey, a wide receiver from Southern University in Louisiana, could field it just behind the goal line.

Winey turned upfield but was stopped in his tracks by Paul Nastasiuk, a reserve Canadian slotback. Winey struggled to move the ball across the goal. But he was downed there in the end zone; and 15–14, on the rouge, the Lions won the game.

Now the noise was thunderous. And the fans appeared clearly Canadian after all. They knew to expect the rouge. This was their game and their League. Here in Canada, it seemed, the CFL was valued and well.

As I traveled around the Canadian Football League, I found that most older fans appreciated the distinctive Canadian brand of football. There was strong loyalty to the Winnipeg Blue Bombers, the Edmonton Eskimos, and the Saskatchewan Roughriders among middle-aged fans.

I was fascinated by the CFL, not just as a professional sports operation but as a national institution. Seventy-five years old, it carried a remarkable tradition.

In Regina, Saskatchewan – a small city isolated out on the Midwestern plains – I visited the Roughriders' headquarters on Saturday morning the day before a big game. Taylor Field is an aging stadium with bright, multicolored stands. It sits in the midst of a blue-collar neighborhood, right next to the railroad yards.

The field was a beehive of peewee-league, "touch" football games that morning. Fathers ran around coaching and refereeing, reveling in the fun as much as their sons.

Across the street, hundreds of fans mobbed the practice field for a photo session after the Riders' workout. The players, in bright emerald jerseys, stood out in the crowd. Fans of all ages – toddlers, teenagers, young adult parents – swarmed the Riders for autographs. There was entertainment for everyone: drawing for prizes, a rock band, and a green-haired clown.

That was the kind of scene I encountered many times throughout the CFL. The Canadian Football League clearly was a serious commercial venture, with big stadiums and payrolls for the players. It was an exchange of goods and services. But, more than a business, it was a cultural event. And not even "culture" in the staid professional sense of hiring paid entertainers. The CFL was a do-it-yourself production put on by communities themselves.

Farmers flocked to pre-game pancake breakfasts on Game Day in Regina. In Winnipeg, head coach Mike Riley and his players drove hours winter weekends across the frozen plains of Manitoba to participate in fund-raiser hockey games with fans. There were beauty contests and Country Western music shows at the Grey Cup.

Gradually it dawned on me that professional football in western Canada was mostly an excuse for people to get together. And I came to understand Canadian culture. It was this ability of people to make connection in ordinary ways – to meet and make meaning through a game they enjoyed. For a man-without-a-tribe like me, the CFL made me proud to be at least an ancestral Canadian. I marveled at the depth of its traditions.

In Saskatchewan they told the story of Vernon Vaughn, a black American defensive back who played for the Roughriders during the 1960s. Vaughn had come from the racially troubled state of Maryland, but he found a home among the Canadians of Regina where there are scarcely any blacks. He loved his association with the fans and players there. Tragically the young man contracted leukemia. When he learned he was dying, he asked to be buried in his Roughriders' uniform. And he was.

Then there was Huck Welch. I heard his tale from his widow at the annual Hall of Fame dinner in Hamilton, Ontario, where they maintain the CFL museum. Welch was inducted to the Hall of Fame as one of the League's greatest punters. But he was remembered for his courage and sense of humor as well.

Late in life, Welch suffered very poor health. Ultimately he'd lost a leg to diabetes. Just before they anesthetized him for the operation, he peered up at his wife and grinned. "Make sure they have plenty of formaldehyde, eh? For a punter like me, they'll wanta preserve my toe."

Later, when he was fatally ill, Huck took his wife aside and made a final request. "Now if anything happens to me, will you go over to the Hall of Fame every once in a while, look up my statue and pat my head."

"So every time I go there," she told me, "maybe once a year, I just stop by his bust and pat him on his head."

Whatever its traditions, however, the Canadian Football League was dying by degrees. Talking with players and fans, coaches and journalists, I soon began to understand why. The CFL was succumbing to electronic communications. The global economy was killing it.

Virtually every fan under thirty had lost interest in the Canadian Football League. Raised on television in a country with 600 cable TV systems, the younger generation had grown up watching the National Football League. Now they all preferred the American four-down game to their own.

The CFL generation gap was apparent all across Canada. In Dawson Creek, British Columbia, out among the WATCH FOR MOOSE signs on the Alaska Highway, there were NFL-Miami Dolphin fans. Everywhere I traveled, it was hard to find a young-adult Canadian Football League enthusiast. Canada's Marshall McLuhan had foretold the coming global village. Now it was real. Televised football had captured the nation's young fans.

In Toronto and Montreal, Canada's large eastern cities, the CFL was losing ground even faster. But here the competition was not so much television as status. In growing cities with world-class aspirations, the Canadian Football League seemed provincial and much too small.

On the shores of Lake Ontario near downtown Toronto, there is a gigantic space needle some 150 stories high. There's a revolving restaurant on top where one can look out hundreds of miles in all directions. But there's not much to see from the tower, and the view is not the point of it. The CN Tower serves one primary function: it is the world's tallest structure.

At the base of the tower stands a great Vulcanian statue, and next to that is the Skydome – the largest sports complex in the world. The stadium opened this summer in the middle of the major league baseball season.

Completed at a cost of 400 million dollars, the Skydome features an instantly retractable roof and a system of refreshment stands so vast that it's managed by McDonald's. There's a 300-foot bar and a luxury hotel where each room has a view of the playing field.

Toronto is like that. The city seems enamored of size. Often as I've been there, I'm still not certain why. Perhaps it's the presence of Americans. Riding down the elevator in the CN Tower, I asked the operator how this structure compared to New York City's Empire State Building. That was the epitome of height when I was a kid.

"It's about three times higher," he said. Then he thought a moment and mused, "You know, it's funny; when I tell Americans that, they often can't believe me. They insist the Empire State Building is taller."

Toronto is rapidly nullifying any American claims to superiority. The city is not only big but liveable in as well. There's a fraction of the crime one would find in an American city of comparable size, such as Philadelphia. People queue up at the bus stops in Toronto. No one sleeps on the streets.

The good life in Toronto may be mostly a matter of money. Toronto always had been an important financial center for English-speaking Canada. But when French-Canadian nationalism swept across Quebec in the late 1960s, hundreds of Anglo firms bolted from Montreal. They settled with their bank accounts in Toronto.

Then in the 1980s another wave of migrants arrived from the Far East. An estimated 30,000 Hong Kong millionaires settled in Toronto, wary of China's intentions when Britain gives up the island in 1997. Countless others may follow after the upheaval at Tiananmen Square.

Some of Toronto's most élite suburbs now are one-third Oriental. Children from Hong Kong excel in the high schools, just as in the

United States. And they suffer the stings of discrimination in a strange land. To resentful Anglo teenagers, the Orientals are FOBs. That's Fresh Off the Boat, in graffiti.

From its elegant symphony hall to its art museum with an entire gallery of Henry Moore sculptures, Toronto has all the accoutrements of a first-class international city. But there's an insidious, restless spirit in Toronto, a craving never wholly satisfied. Toronto's a great city, it seems to say. But are we good enough?

I came across this clothier's ad in the Toronto *Globe and Mail* and had to read it twice. At first I thought it was a joke.

> DATELINE PARIS – Right now, you're probably saying to yourself: "He's in Europe again? This must be the fifth time this year!" ... Well, not quite the fifth, but I do seem to spend a lot of time abroad ... I come to see the shows – SEHM here in Paris, Pitti Uomo and others in Italy. There are simply no better fashion forums in the world. We're talking seminal men's style ...
>
> I do so much traveling during the year that certain places seem like "homes away from home." One such place is the Madison Hotel on Boulè St Germain. Comfortable, friendly, and very conveniently located in the heart of the city, the Madison rates five stars in Saul Korman's Baedecker. And I mustn't forget my favourite overseas carrier: Air Canada, which takes me to and from the fashion centres in first-class style ...

The ad says a lot about the egotism of Saul Korman, not to mention his resourcefulness. The commercial plugs probably garner free air fare and lodging. But it speaks to his readership, too, and their need for validation. People who would purchase clothing from someone like this must have something to prove. They want to be up-to-date on an international scale. The proper arena for Toronto seems to be the world. Toronto is a far cry from the simple pleasures of CFL cities in the West. It's an environment where the future of the League appears doubtful at best.

I saw the Toronto Argonauts play the last game of their regular season on a raw, foggy Sunday in November 1987. This was back in the days before the Skydome with its retractable roof. It was a day to test the sinuses, and no more than 10,000 fans had ventured out to the 50,000-seat Exhibition Stadium on the lake.

The Argos were playing Winnipeg's Blue Bombers. It was a close, dramatic game. With time running out, the Argos trailed the

Bombers by a single point. Lance Chomyc, the Toronto kicker, had accounted for all his team's scoring. But he'd missed his last field goal attempt. Now, with the ball near mid-field, Chomyc approached head coach Bob O'Billovich and asked for a chance to win the game.

O'Billovich had the option of sending in the League's top punter, Hank Ilesic, to try for a one-point "rouge" – kicking the ball past the goal line and preventing a runback as Lui Passaglia had done to defeat the Blue Bombers in Vancouver. But Chomyc looked intent on the field goal, and his coach agreed to let him try it.

In the press conference after the game, it was determined that Chomyc had never kicked a field goal this long. But he hit the ball square at the fifty-yard line, and it carried through the mist floating just above the crossbar for a 20–18 victory.

The crowd by now was very thin: one section on the thirty yard line was populated solely by seagulls, each in a chair of its own. Yet the diehard fans made a lot of noise. They clattered empty seats, wailing "Aaargohhs . . ." Those who had come out for the game on a day like this still clearly cared about their team.

But they weren't enough to support the franchise. In recent years the Argos have suffered one-million-dollar annual losses. That would have been unheard-of in the past. Till a decade ago, the Argonauts had a loyal contingent of fans. The team is steeped in English-Canadian tradition. It originated in the nineteenth century as an off-season rugby organization for members of an exclusive collegiate rugby club. The Argonauts' light and dark blue uniforms represented the colors of Oxford and Cambridge Universities. Like most CFL franchises, the Argos had been owned by a group of fans in the community.

In recent years a large Canadian brewery, Carling O'Keefe, owned the team and took the losses. Curiously, Carling's didn't seem much interested in marketing the Argonauts. Of course there was no question of sponsoring amateur hockey games and pancake breakfasts. Not in a place like Toronto where culture is for specialists like Henry Moore. But neither was there any other kind of promotion. All around the League people wondered about Carling's intentions. "What's their game plan?"

Then, just after the 1988 Grey Cup in Ottawa, the Argos called a sudden press conference with a shocking announcement. Elders IXL, the Australian brewers of Foster's Lager and parent company of Carling O'Keefe, had decided to divest itself of its two North

American sports franchises: the football Argonauts and a National Hockey League team, the Quebec Nordiques.

Quebecers reacted fast; hockey is serious business to French Canadians. Marcel Aubut, the Nordiques' president, had caught wind of the sale two weeks before. It was rumored that the prospective buyer of the Nordiques was an Anglo-Canadian and/or American who had thoughts of moving the team to Hamilton, Ontario, or even across the border. Aubut assembled a group of local businesses who purchased the team and secured it in Quebec City.

In Toronto the response to this multinational deal was muddled and slow. The Argos had been sold to Harry Ornest, a wealthy Canadian expatriate who has lived for the past twenty-five years in Beverly Hills, California. Ornest is a veteran sports franchise owner who once saved the NHL St Louis Blues when they were about to move to Saskatoon, Saskatchewan in Canada. Ornest seemed a world-class entrepreneur fit for Toronto. It was he who had tried to buy the Nordiques.

Toronto's newspapers were filled with conjecture over Ornest's intentions. In buying the Argonauts he'd also acquired exclusive football rights for the new Skydome. Should the Canadian Football League collapse after eighteen months, Ornest could insert a National Football League team in the Skydome. Owing to the NFL's various legal entanglements and other American cities competing for franchises, it seemed doubtful that the US league would be coming to Toronto very soon. But Ornest could afford to wait. Now he held exclusive, long-term rights to football in the Skydome.

The timing of all these transactions was ironic, for the CFL had just completed one of its most successful championship games in history. In the long Canadian tradition of "regional equalization,' distributing income and other resources wherever they were needed, the CFL teams had staged a successful championship game at the site of their weakest franchise. The Grey Cup probably had saved the Ottawa Rough Riders.

But the Ottawa Grey Cup may have signaled the end of an era – a time when CFL teams would look out for one another in the same spirit of commonweal that had repeatedly held the country itself together. Now it seemed that the future of the League had been negotiated by a California millionaire and a multinational corporation in Australia. "What's their game plan?" For a city so immersed in the global economy, it was a question somewhat larger than the CFL.

Fascinating as I found all these social developments, I was interested in their impact on the individual players as well. The career counselor in me wondered about their futures. I spent some time with Lance Chomyc, the Toronto kicker, the morning after the team was sold. If I hadn't arranged to meet him in the locker room, I'd not have recognized Lance as a professional athlete. He's a small, wiry fellow with thick-lensed glasses.

Lance is as much an intellectual as the spectacles imply: an honors graduate in English from the University of Toronto. His father directs the guidance and counseling program in Edmonton, Alberta's secondary schools. His mother heads a medical research lab. "My family has more degrees than a thermometer," Lance says. He's begun working on a graduate degree in English and plans a career in college teaching.

Chomyc grew up in Edmonton, out on the western plains. Like most young Canadians, he hadn't played organized football till the tenth grade in high school. He discovered his kicking abilities as a goalkeeper in soccer. The first time he kicked the ball out of goal, it carried far downfield. That's when the football coach recruited him as a place kicker.

With the longer field and a slightly rounder ball, kicking is somewhat different in Canada from the States. There's more emphasis here on distance, one has a fraction of a second longer to get off a kick, and they use a small tee in Canada. Canadian kickers often exceed the distances of Americans. But because of the games' slight differences, their skills are not directly transferable to the States.

With the rules passed on from rugby, kickers are more important in Canada. Many games are decided by kicking for field position, and sometimes for the rouge. Chomyc shares a strong sense of fraternity with the other Canadian kickers. His teammate, Hank Ilesic, is perhaps the greatest punter in the history of the CFL.

But Lance hears the echoes of empty stands in Toronto. Regardless of how much he loves his game, he's begun to consider what the deafening indifference to Canadian football in Toronto portends for his career. Last year, his long-time friend Dean Dorsey had a tryout with the Green Bay Packers of the NFL. He lasted only a few games; the transition to American kicking was more than he could manage. But this year Hank Ilesic made the NFL team in San Diego.

Then there's Lui Passaglia, now nearing the end of his career at the age of thirty-four. Lui is a lifelong CFL fan as well. He grew up wanting nothing more than to build a life in Vancouver and play for the hometown BC Lions. "You mean you never considered moving to the NFL?" I asked him one morning. "Weren't you attracted to the salaries they offer?" He looked at me with wonder: "Have you ever seen Vancouver?" Last year, however, the BC Lions almost went bankrupt. Salaries were cut as attendance fell and the League declined. Ten players quit the team. Lui became discouraged. He went down for a tryout with the NFL Cleveland Browns. As it turned out, by then it was too late to move.

"I'm thirty-four now," he reflected, "at the twilight of my career. The Browns were never seriously interested in me. They let me kick in their third exhibition game. Then they kept a twenty-six-year-old guy instead." Passaglia came back home by default.

Next year, if his leg and the League hold up, Lui may be back for one more season. He wonders now about his retirement. Not so much making a living. He's tried his hand as a stockbroker, and there's the option of teaching high school.

It seems his questions have as much to do with the future of the Canadian Football League as his own career. That's where he spent thirteen years of his life and achieved his fame.

I think about that, too. When Lui Passaglia kicked a fifty-three-yard punt with a four-second hang time to defeat the Winnipeg Blue Bombers in the final seconds of play on 30 August 1987, I was in the crowd. It was the first rouge and one of the greatest kicks I ever saw.

I wrote an article about that game in *The Christian Science Monitor* and gave a copy to Lui. He paused in the middle of a press session and took time to read it. Passaglia recognizes that any time now the CFL and all of its traditions may be forgotten. "What's a rouge?" another generation of Canadian kids will say.

None of this is lost on Lance Chomyc, who at the age of twenty-five has an entire athletic career in front of him. Should he skip to the NFL when his contract expires this year? The Canadian game has been his whole frame of reference in football. But it's floundering.

Lance and his wife spend a lot of time considering career decisions. He shakes his head, looking around the Argonauts' locker room. "This is all I ever wanted to do," he says. "I dreamed of playing football in the CFL . . . If we could just afford to buy a house."

In Carl Sagan's book on human evolution, *Dragons of Eden*, there's a memorable comment on mythological beasts: all those quasi-human creatures our ancestors remembered and feared so. Sagan believes that creatures something like that existed. They were preserved in fear and memory because of all the anguish human beings went through, killing them off.

I wonder if cultural evolution is like that. Take an institution just a little bit different, like the Canadian Football League. Add a larger neighbor, say, the United States: numerous and powerful enough to set the norms. If the smaller institution has a modicum of distance, it probably can preserve its character and maintain a following of local supporters. However simple the institution and its gatherings, some people will find meaning there. It will be part of their culture.

But set that institution next to another, much larger and almost like it – a National Football League, for example: a League with a billion-dollar budget that now plays exhibition games in England and soon will have an affiliate in Europe.

Saturate CFL fans with the larger league on television. Inundate them with NFL football. Soon you'll have a cultural version of *Dragons of Eden* all over again. With electronic technology shrinking distance, differences become deviations. Mass markets make for homogeneous norms, universal icons just like Michael Jackson.

In the whole global question of cultural survival, the place where Lance Chomyc finds himself is surely not so bad. The prospective loss of Canadian professional football does not rank with, say, the plight of Manute Bol's Dinkas in the southern Sudan where children are sold into slavery.

But the slow decline of the Canadian Football League is one more instance of local culture giving way to global commerce. It's giving up occasions where plain people have gathered and shared something meaningful. It's a loss of tribal spirit.

Serge Amyot, football writer for the *Journal du Montréal*, takes a different perspective on the circumstances of the CFL. To him they seem much less tragic. Serge is a bright, intense individual who's not at all reluctant to share his views. Around the League, they call him "the coach."

I spent a late-autumn afternoon in Montreal with him, learning about French Canadians and their tastes in sports. I was curious why the Montreal franchise, the Alouettes, had folded one week before the 1988 CFL season. And I had personal interests in Montreal as well.

To the extent that I can claim any single ethnic heritage, it's probably French Canadian. My great-grandfather, whose ring I wear, was a supreme court justice in Quebec. My father's cousin is a nun who spent decades of her life teaching English to French-speaking rural Quebecers. Her brother served thirty-four years as clerk of the Manitoba Legislature. There's a sense of family history in Quebec. I found a full page of 350 Charlands in the Montreal phone book.

But the French Canadians are a foreign lot to me. I am one of millions of Canadian-Americans whose ancestors shed their culture as they migrated south. My father left Ottawa looking for work at the age of twenty, when his father lost his political job with Prime Minister Wilfred Laurier; he never looked back. So many who left Quebec saw their ethnic roots as something to be rid of. I myself have learned some Greek and Hebrew, Spanish and Swahili because of certain work I wanted to do. But never French. That would have required some feeling for my heritage.

It was my son Jay who sparked my interest when he took a Canadian history course in college several years ago. "The French Canadians succeeded in preserving their culture," he concluded. "But from what I can tell, there was nothing in their culture worth preserving." I resolved to take at least a quick look for myself, through the CFL history in Montreal.

The Alouettes, I learned, had been caught in the throes of French Canadian politics during their years in Montreal. Their fortunes had fallen with the rising militancy of the Parti Quebecois and the flight of Anglos to Toronto.

Traditionally Montreal's football fans had been mostly English-speakers. Gradually, however, the owners of the Alouettes recognized they had a different clientele with distinctive tastes on their hands. They learned that French Canadian fans appreciate anything done with flair. They like to watch world-class events. And they care only for winners.

Canadian football tried to cater to the international pretensions of Montreal fans. The owners imported a half-dozen star players from the National Football League, at enormous expense, to foster a major league image. That was the undoing of the franchise.

The all-star team was a disaster on the field. Canadian football requires unique skills that don't quite conform to the American game. French Canadian fans quickly deserted the team, and the Alouettes franchise folded.

But as the CFL sun was setting in Montreal, French Canada was preoccupied with other opportunities. In the 1970s, Montreal journalist René Levesque stumbled upon an intriguing story while investigating a new hydroelectric project under construction in northern Quebec. Most of the power from the new plant was designated for the New England region of the United States. And it seemed that most of the contracts for constructing the facility were headed there, too.

That was a familiar story to the man who would become leader of the Parti Quebecois. French Canadians occupied a kind of "painless purgatory" in North America where Anglophones made basic decisions.

Levesque convinced the Quebecers that their centuries-long second-class citizenship could end. If they could mobilize politically, it would be possible to generate a new, independent economy based on selling hydroelectric power to the United States. Quebec did indeed win a new measure of economic and political freedom.

Serge Amyot saw the rejection of Canadian football as part of that larger story. It was one more instance of the Quebecers' resolute drive for independence. They weren't about to conform to the popular culture of English Canadians any more.

I asked him how he felt about some of the Canadian Football League's English Canadian traditions, such as the Hall of Fame Dinner I'd attended where the guests of honor marched in behind a bagpiper and everyone stood to toast the Queen.

That got him started. "They're talking about their Queen, which is the Queen of England! There is really no Canadian institution," he exclaimed.

He recounted many instances of discrimination he had experienced as a French Canadian: being relegated to the back row of the press box in Winnipeg; a general sense of derogation by the other sportswriters whenever he appeared to cover a game.

"For me," he said, "CFL represent absolutely nothing! I'm still a stranger. My identity is as a Quebecer, not as a Canadian." (Angered, he spoke faster than his English.) "I feel as stranger in Toronto that I feel in Chicago. There is no difference for me. More than that, when I'm going to the Grey Cup, I feel like a trouble-maker. 'Here come the Froggy! Here come the guy who's bitching all the time.'"

"But when I'm going to the Super Bowl (the NFL championship

game) it's 'Here come a reporter!' I don't want to be treated differently because I'm French and from Montreal. I'd rather be a normal reporter in Dallas than a minority reporter in Regina. In the NFL, I'm just one of the boys."

I took notes furiously all afternoon, caught up in this French Canadian's spirit – in the excitement of contact with a tradition my family had abandoned in Quebec. Now I believed that I understood the essential need of the French Canadians to claim their own land and culture. Of course they had to look beyond English Canada. Only with an independent economic and political base could they meet others as equals. Truly the province of Quebec was the world.

A stray word in French came back to me: *engage*! That was Serge, all right. This man was engaged with the causes of his time, quite unlike the laconic reserve I sometimes found among English Canadians. *Engage*: he cared enough about the Canadian Football League to despise it. I remembered some of these same qualities in my father and his French cousin in Winnipeg. For the first time, I began to identify with this part of my history.

Yet even as I was leaving the *Journal du Montréal* I found myself remembering my son's sophomoric conclusion. Was there a French Canadian culture, some way of life these people wished to share with the rest of the world? Or did they simply wish to join it? I could appreciate Serge Amyot's enthusiasm for the new global village. But a comment of his kept recurring.

"I just got back from a trip to the Netherlands," he'd exulted. "There are no borders now! Everywhere you go, you find a McDonald's."

8 · *High-Tech Futures*

In the end, of course, I had to learn that you can't adopt a tribe. The lesson wasn't long coming. I'd wandered down toward St Laurent Street, a kind of boundary to the rougher, French part of town where Anglos didn't venture. I wanted a closer look at the neighborhood near Olympic Stadium where I'd been told some fans were afraid to go. Had that also hurt the Alouettes?

At first glance the area didn't look bad. Nothing like the ghettos of Atlanta or Chicago. There was a small delicatessen where I stopped to pick up some Quebec wine and cheese for friends in Toronto.

Standing with my purchase at the cash register, I asked the clerk how much it came to. He gave the price in French. I smiled and shrugged. He frowned and then, as to a child, began to trace out numbers in the air.

I took a step forward and fixed him with a stare: "I don't speak French," I said slowly.

He knew some English: "You should have told me."

I moved to the counter: "I didn't know that was necessary."

"No problem!"the manager intervened, fluent in English. He rang up the sale. "You come back! Have a nice day!"

I stood there for a moment and stared at the Quebecers with my best urban American bravado.

"Be cool," I admonished, and walked away.

So much for kinship in Quebec. As I drove out of town down St Laurent Street, I felt as empty and alien as ever.

"You get to choose your home," said the young woman from Ireland as she left her parents' home in England for Australia. Perhaps the other side of that observation is that you have to.

For a long time, I've recognized that my essential roots are spiritual. I suppose that's what Jesus meant when he seemed to discount his blood relatives: "Who is my mother . . .?" Each of us must choose those who might help us find our way in life.

My basic forebears lived in seventeenth-century England at the very end of the Reformation. That was a trying time when Christians were exhausted from a century of conflict in the church. Several groups essentially gave up attempting to reform existing religious structures and systems of thought. They started new spiritual movements of their own.

Some of these Christian rebels were quietists who rejected not just religious dogma but every rationalized world-view they found. They thought no more of Enlightenment philosophers than of Anglican creeds.

Isaac Penington, an early Quaker, was a wealthy aristocrat who withdrew from society to devote himself to a slow and careful quest for wisdom. His writings combine biblical faith with a quiet Eastern spirit very much like Zen Buddhism.

"Give over thine own willing," wrote Penington, "give over thine own running, give over thine own desiring to know or be anything and sink down to the seed which God sows in thy heart, and let that be in thee and grow in thee and breathe in thee and act in thee."

Many of these Nonconformists suffered from their loss of formal faith. Both Isaac Penington and George Fox, who founded the Quakers, would probably be categorized as chronic depressives today. Their journals are filled with episodes of despondence as they contended with frightful spirits in the process of reworking their faith.

"I fasted much, and walked abroad in solitary places many days, and often took my Bible and went and sat in hollow trees and lonesome places till night came on . . ." Fox wrote of his youth. "When it was day I wished for night, and when it was night I wished for day."

Still the Quakers continued to cast off every sort of religious convention. "I resolved never to go back to those things I have left, having discovered death and darkness to be in them; but would rather be without a religion, until the Lord taught me one," Isaac Penington's wife Mary said.

In the course of his wanderings, Fox came in contact with another group of dissidents known simply as the Seekers. These individuals had also given up organized religion. Yet they still had spiritual needs. They determined to meet regularly for worship, but in silence. Only when one of them felt personally inspired would she or he engage in any sort of preaching.

Fox found new life and a spiritual home among the Seekers. As "Quakers" (a derogatory term based on the behavior of some of them in court) they experienced fresh leadings of the Spirit and new disciplines to build spiritual maturity.

Quakers kept journals to chart their inward journeys, often with remarkable candor. They learned to "center down" – sitting quietly in the presence of confusion, or doubt, or temptation – rather than rush toward some premature solution to a problem of morality or belief.

As the radical Reformers formed new bonds of fellowship and stable communities of faith, they sensed more and more "openings" in the spiritual darkness surrounding them. Fox discovered that beyond his personal "ocean of darkness there was an ocean of light." He found inner strength and courage to take action on his faith.

Others such as William Penn were born activists. Penn was a character to be reckoned with. The son of a British Lord Admiral, he was a rambunctious individual in his own right. Once when he was brought to trial for preaching illegally and possibly fomenting a riot, he called out to his jury from the defendant's dock: "You are Englishmen; mind your privilege, give not away your right."

"Nor will we ever do it," the foreman replied. Sometimes it wasn't easy for reformers such as Penn to distinguish themselves from other rabble-rousers like the Ranters who were mostly bent on protest *per se*. Later he would write: "True godliness does not turn men out of the world, but enables them to live better in it and excites their endeavors to mend it."

Penn followed his vision overseas, where he used a royal land grant given to his father to found the colony of Pennsylvania. The Pilgrims, another group of radical Reformers, founded a North American colony of their own at Massachusetts Bay. It's hard to overestimate the influence of these independent idealists in shaping the subsequent course of American history.

But many of them paid dearly for their ventures in faith. A whole colony of Puritans went mad over witchcraft in the wilderness of New England. They were done in by the influence of Caribbean voodoo spirit-worship practiced by their slaves.

Whether active or contemplative, the religious radicals of seventeenth-century England constantly wrestled with anarchy. They understood what testing the spirits meant. To me, that's the timeless value of the Quakers and Pilgrims. Not the content of their beliefs, which they were always revising anyway, but the existential process of their seeking. I value the way their faith was formed.

There was a refreshing realism about these seekers. They recognized, just as Jesus, that they lived in a world full of diverse spirits. They knew that spirits roil in the heart of every human life. They're pervasive spirits, and very confusing. Some can lift you up, and others bring you down.

The worst thing one might do was to underestimate the spirits' power, explaining them away through the illusion of some single truth. The best course was to attend to all of the spirits, around you and within. Attend to your complexity. Test the spirits for the source of life.

But these people also understood their fundamental need for community. It was in fellowship with one another that they grew to find the substance of their faith, not wandering in isolation like the young George Fox.

The Pilgrims assembled on board ship, right on the heels of their perilous voyage across the Atlantic, and joined in the Mayflower Compact: "We covenant with the Lord and with one another and do bind ourseves to walk together in all His ways known or to be made known, what-so-ever it may cost us."

The Pilgrims would evolve into Congregationalists, committed to local governance in church affairs. The Quakers organized themselves as Meetings, for the same reason. In the midst of all their journeying, they understood that every venture of faith begins in primary relationships. Faith is formed from the spirits of one's time and place. Faith begins at home.

That was the way I came back to concentrate on life in America. I was no less fascinated by the spirits of other places, and just as intrigued by the possibilities I saw around the world. But my journey needed grounding. I came back to seek the emerging global economy in the United States.

There was a new think-tank in town, the Center for the New

West. It was intended to work at strategies for economic development in the West. I decided to try affiliating with them, exploring some of the same approaches I'd seen in Enterprise Scotland and among the *jua kali* of Kenya. They sent me to a conference of university research park directors out in California, to gather some material for an article on economic development and academic research.

San Francisco is a crossroads for the spirits of America. I remembered it as a beautiful area from a visit in my teens. Now it had become one of the leading high-technology centers in the world.

The conference was held at the San Francisco Hilton Hotel, downtown near Union Square. It was an occasion full of uplifting experiences – erudite lectures on high technology and global economics, and an elegant reception on the thirty-second floor of the Westin St Francis Hotel.

I found myself in a cluster of scientists at the reception, half listening to their jargon while gazing off across the skyline. A couple of physicists were discussing "conceptual patents." A bank of clouds was looming up from the Bay.

As the clouds rose, they began to float towards us. Gradually they engulfed our tower, obliterating the world outside. Now we were confined to our conversations; my attention turned to patent law.

Then the clouds parted and drifted inland as inexorably as they'd come. Back came the sunshine and the breathtaking sights of San Francisco, the City by the Bay.

Downstairs a string quartet played Schubert for cocktails in the lobby. There's a lot to be said for conferences at luxury hotels, and this was one of the headiest I'd ever attended. What a rarefied view of the world you could cultivate from here!

As long as you stayed inside. The streets of San Francisco were an assault to the senses: a seething caldron of contemporary life. Step outside the St Francis and you were inundated with pornography on an incredible scale: shops and shows pandering to every sort of pain and vice. "Hard core!!" "Talk to a naked woman for one minute: $5.00." "Girls, Girls, Girls." "Men, Men, Men."

There were droves of homeless people, most of them pathetic beggars. But others were deranged and aggressive. They reeled along the sidewalks, screaming obscenities into the air. Some seemed bent on accosting anyone who resembled a tourist.

It seemed there were denizens of every Oriental culture filtering into America through the dregs of street life in San Francisco. One young man from South East Asia attacked another Oriental. He chased him with a sharpened screwdriver till they came in sight of a police car. Then he turned to face off against a park fence, as if to attack it instead. The young man swayed in the menacing dance of some crazed martial art. As the police car drove slowly toward him, he vanished into the crowd.

Mostly there were great numbers of young Japanese, all of them in blue jeans, with cameras. Some held video recorders. I watched them as I walked back to the hotel from dinner and wondered why they would leave the safety of their islands to visit a place like this. I did understand why they traveled in groups.

I'd spent the evening with some East Coast scientists and found myself mulling over some of their stories from Japan.

One fellow from Atlanta, Georgia, where they have a new international airport, told of meeting a Japanese businessman. He was shocked to find that the Japanese had heard of his southern state.

"Well, I'll be danged. We were told that airport would put us on the map," he'd marveled.

"What airport?" said the Japanese. "Isn't Georgia where they filmed *Gone with the Wind*?"

Then there was the story of Americans touring biotechnology labs in Japan. One scientific marvel followed another. It was an experience as surreal as *Godzilla*, the Japanese science-fiction film. The Americans were feeling a bit overwhelmed as they came to another laboratory filled with seaweed. Racks of kelp hung from the ceiling. Some of the stuff was twelve feet long.

"In this lab we grow kelp very big, very fast," the guide explained.

"Hey, I saw that movie," an American quipped. The others collapsed in stifled laughter.

Out on the street with the Japanese, I wondered what stories they told of us. It occurred to me they might not be humorous. One of them had stopped to film a vagrant on his cardboard bed.

Conferences in America are mostly serious business, nothing like the old-boys' conventions where people just got drunk and rowdy in the past. Today conferencing is an industry with an annual budget the size of higher education. There's still some carousing that goes on, to be sure. Somebody is patronizing the porn shops. But professional conferences are more and more genuine educational events. In a society where state-of-the-art knowledge lasts only about three years, they're a vital means of continuing education.

The research park directors turned out to be mostly a group of commercial real estate managers. Their past meetings had focused on practical questions of their trade: tenant relations, property appraisals, and the like. But in the last several years the field had changed markedly. Universities were forming much closer relationships with businesses, to market the products of academic research. These real-estate specialists had a lot to catch up on.

Relationships of colleges with capitalists are nothing new. Schools have wooed wealthy donors for centuries, through stratagems such as honorary diplomas. Samuel Johnson cynically observed St Andrews "getting richer by degrees."

Donors still endow professorial chairs and put up buildings in honor of themselves or family members. Economist Milton Friedman quips that American higher education seems engaged in two industries: knowledge and immortality. Colleges cater to wealth in order to survive.

But today a new kind of business-education relationship is burgeoning. It's a more equal and ambitious alliance than in the past, and quite a lot more passionate. Chase Peterson, President of the University of Utah, calls it "academic capitalism." The new partnership is based on buying and selling academic research.

In a global economy caught in rampant change, modern industry needs an affordable source of basic research. Companies like Hewlett-Packard, with its two-year-old products, require constant research. When it comes to new technology, nothing fits the bill like academia. Steve Gomes, a leader in the research park movement, observes: "The university is the factory of the future."

Academic capitalism is a worldwide movement. Even the San Francisco conference of US research park directors had an international flavor. Seventeen nations sent delegates, and a Canadian was elected president of the American association.

The Irish president of an international research park association turned up as well. They're to hold a joint convention with the American group next year. Michael Ryan was a congenial fellow from Limerick who brought gifts of Irish crystal and proposed that the two associations develop a program of international home exchange.

While he meant well, Ryan was not entirely at home with

American ways. He gave a luncheon address larded with crude sexist jokes that made his audience squirm.

But when it came to describing his own university research park, which now spawns ten new high-tech companies every year, his message came through loud and clear. Ryan spoke to the Americans about "small business incubators, seed funds, intellectual property, academic entrepreneurship, technology transfer," and they understood him well.

He gave the same spiel on a radio interview, and the director of economic development in metropolitan Los Angeles called in long-distance from his car phone to arrange a breakfast meeting. The language of economic development was as universal as the concept of commercializing academic research. "Knowledge-as-enterprise" was spoken everywhere.

The technology transfer movement began at Stanford, down the peninsula from San Francisco, just after World War II. The university at that time was a strong intellectual center with a weak financial base. Founded in the late nineteenth century by a merchant who'd grown wealthy from the Gold Rush, Stanford's modern endowment barely met its needs.

The school had a modest five-million-dollar annual budget in the mid-1940s and a student body of 2500. The average salary for full professors was $8000 a year. Then suddenly, as the war ended, Stanford was overrun with returning veterans. In two years enrollment swelled to 8200. The school was pressed to respond to its new role in the post-war world.

Stanford found it had two resources that were underutilized: its property and its people. According to the terms of Leland Stanford's will the 8200-acre estate could not be sold. But the land might be put to new uses. A soil analysis determined that not much of it was suited for farming. What else might they do?

About that time, Frederick Terman became dean of the engineering school. Terman turned out to be a rare hybrid: both an academician and a dyed-in-the-wool entrepreneur. He used the university's strong physics department to generate government and industry research contracts.

Then he helped found the nation's first university-affiliated research park. The Stanford Industrial Park was a gamble for a school in somewhat dire straits. The first tenant firm was persuaded to design its manufacturing facility in the form of an elementary school, so that it could be converted if the business venture failed. Varian Electronics occupies the same red brick building today – a corporate headquarters with schoolroom windows, a low sloping roof, and a flagpole in the parking lot.

Other universities followed Stanford's suit. In North Carolina, three schools teamed with the state government to create an industrial park close to the University of North Carolina, North Carolina State, and Duke. The North Carolina Research Triangle attracted major corporations and contributed significantly to economic recovery in the state.

Traditionally, most universities' ventures into private industry emanated from personal relationships. They required people who were comfortable in both business and academic environments, and whom both communities trusted. Individuals such as Stanford's Fred Terman were key to technology transfer.

In one instance a Harvard biology professor was sent to call on a whisky distiller for a donation to the university's building fund. During lunch the conversation turned to biomedical factors in alcoholism – a subject the corporate executives found intriguing. At the end of the day the professor left without a donation to the building fund, but with a grant to study alcoholism instead.

The same kind of story can be told many times: faculty members collaborating with researchers in private industry, scientists alternating jobs in both fields. A dentist in Fort Collins, Colorado, teamed with an engineering professor at Colorado State University. Together they came up with WaterPik: a jet-stream device for cleaning teeth. Other Colorado State researchers developed Viadent, a toothpaste that combats gum disease, from a local Indian medicine. It's manufactured today in a small plant just off campus.

Joint ventures between businesses and universities flourished naturally. If there were any sort of controversy to technology transfer in the old days, it came up mostly in connection with defense research. Stanford was plagued with demonstrations during the Vietnam War era; the university still ranks fifth in the nation for defense contracting.

It was not until the 1980s Reagan decade that American universities entered private industry research full tilt. The reasons were economic rather than philosophical. America was losing ground steadily in the global market place, and the nation's fiscal condition was turning sour.

The problems had begun with a series of "entitlement" programs enacted during the costly Vietnam War. Lyndon Johnson's "guns and butter" budgets had hamstrung the federal budget, and mortgaged the nation's future for decades to come. The number of Americans eligible for benefits such as Social Security had doubled during the 1960s, as expenditures rose 255%.

Today, almost ninety per cent of the US federal budget is consumed by direct payments to individuals, defense expenditures, and servicing the national debt. Debt payments doubled during the 1980s. The federal government continues to fund half the sponsored research in the nation's universities, two-thirds of it for defense. But those funds are increasingly uncertain. Even defense contracts are in jeopardy as Reagan's Star Wars funding is curtailed.

Between the years 1976 and 1987, according to a study by the US National Conference of State Legislatures, *per capita* funding for higher education decreased from ninety-seven cents to ninety-two cents. At the same time, spending for health care under Medicaid increased from thirty-five cents to fifty-eight cents. Expenditures for police and prisons rose from nineteen cents to thirty-three cents. With federal funding in decline, most universities have found themselves turning to academic capitalism by default.

Stanford President Donald Kennedy spoke to the research park managers on management issues in commercial research. Kennedy is a professorial-looking biologist with a good head for business. He appreciates the "demand pull" of applications on academic research. Kennedy believes that universities need the same benefits of reality testing that teaching hospitals have provided medical schools. The prospect of commercial application, turning out a real product, focuses the efforts of researchers and grounds them in reality.

This was familiar language and welcome news to technology transfer specialists. It's the same Tory ethic of Margaret Thatcher, Michael Ryan, and Ronald Reagan: the enterprise culture of our time. What's remarkable is the degree to which this profit ethic has permeated the universities.

I was caught by one of Kennedy's remarks. In reviewing proposals for new research at Stanford, he said, he considers two criteria. The first is whether the research will enhance the university's academic program. The second is whether it will maximize return on endowment.

Driving around Stanford, I wondered about the business of increasing endowment. It was hard to imagine that Stanford needed funds. Palo Alto is less than an hour from San Francisco, but it seems eons off in a luxury all its own.

The university's 12,000 students luxuriate in their 8000-acre campus: two-thirdss of an acre apiece. The campus is a matched set of terra-cotta roofs in a cornucopia of plants and trees: bottle brush, eucalyptus, redwood, oak, and magnolia. Even the research park with its seventy-seven tenant firms looks like an arboretum. The football stadium is enshrouded in ivy.

The beauty of the university has enhanced the value of its environs, and not just in aesthetics. Stanford is an idyllic spot in a land where Nirvanas don't come cheap. College Terrace is a two-block-wide residential neighborhood that separates the research park from the university itself. It's a pleasant section of modest, post-war homes. I noticed a small, three-bedroom bungalow for sale, and asked the price. It was $545,000!

Los Alto Heights is another attractive neighborhood, full of blossoming shrubs and trees. There's a good view to the east from that part of town, across the campus toward the rolling, forested foothills. But just short of the mountains, a thick, polluted cloud bank hovered above the trees. I asked about the clouds.

When Stanford research began to prosper, it was evident there was need for a place to manufacture products such as the new semiconductor. Land-use covenants prohibited expansion into Palo Alto, so the tenant firms looked east.

Santa Clara Valley was a region of dairy farms and orchards so beautiful that when the fruit trees were flowering, buses of tourists would come down from San Francisco just to spend the day. Santa Clara Valley was an idyllic spot. But orchard by orchard, farm by farm, the valley was for sale.

In the course of four decades, the entrepreneurs of a new electronics industry bought up Santa Clara Valley. Gradually they converted it to a barren land of manufacturing plants and parking lots. It's known as "Silicon Valley" today.

I'd noticed it already on the flight in, as the plane descended into San Francisco. As you fly high above the emerald mountains of northern California, gazing down on Redwood Estates settled in the pines, Silicon Valley appears as a shocking, tasteless joke. The valley is a moonscape, like a post-war American suburban shopping center writ large. Silicon Valley is a nightmare of high-tech industry where life ends in asphalt. It is engineers re-creating the world.

9 · *Confusing Fusion*

The effects of high-tech industrial development are beginning to mottle the entire San Francisco Bay. In addition to paving over the natural environment, electronics companies spilled tons of toxic chemicals. IBM faces a million-dollar bill to mop up solvents used to clean electronic parts. Even Stanford's pristine research park is polluted. Environmental studies have found contaminants in one-fifth of the industrial sites.

Here and there among the research park scientists, one heard early echoes of mounting concern over what the universities had got themselves into. A few bad stories had made the national press. There was the University of Rochester's affair with Eastman Kodak, the school's largest donor.

Those two institutions are as intertwined as any in the United States. Most of Kodak's basic research takes place at the University of Rochester, and numerous Kodak employees teach and study there. The case materials used in the university's College of Business come largely from Kodak corporate files.

Two years ago, an employee in the marketing division of Fuji Films, a Japanese competitor of Kodak, applied for admission to the university's Master of Business Administration program. His application was rejected, not because he was unqualified (UR officials got him admitted to a far more prestigious school, the Massachusetts Insitute of Technology), but because of his employment with a major competitor. The prospective student appeared to be a potential industrial spy.

Washington University in St Louis, Missouri, bought into a different kind of compromise with Monsanto chemicals. The university accepted a 23-million-dollar donation to its medical school in return for offering Monsanto exclusive market rights to its research. Under the agreement, the corporation (which created the Vietnam War chemical weapon, Agent Orange) could withhold scientific data for a period of four years while determining its commercial value.

"Intellectual property" became a big issue in the 1980s. More and more, universities found themselves occupied not with the generation of new knowledge but with questions of who owned it. Every institution involved with research had an on-site specialist in patent law. Within a fifteen-year period, membership in the American Association of University Patent Administrators increased seven-fold.

Ironically, most of the leading universities in the profit race were the wealthiest schools, such as Stanford, with a billion-and-a-half dollar endowment, that appeared to need the money least. Johns Hopkins, in Baltimore, Maryland, a major American center for medical research, set up a $500-million commercial research park to market biotech products from the university's research. The facility is expected to generate up to 8000 jobs in Baltimore and annual tax revenues of $3 million. Now in its fifth year of operation, the corporation already has annual revenues of $21 million and a staff of 1700.

James McComas, who heads the Dome Corporation, was interviewed by one of the Baltimore papers. "With all its endowments and grants, why does Hopkins need a 'for-profit' division?" the reporter asked. "To remain in the forefront of science and technology and in health care delivery," replied McComas, "it's a very, very expensive thing to do."

Harvard, the nation's wealthiest university with a four-billion-dollar endowment, has marketed products through its Business School for some time. I know, because somehow I've got on their mailing list. One recent promotion featured videotapes on using information technology as a "competitive weapon." The tapes included an interview with Donald Burr, ex-president of a defunct airline, People Express. Burr was pictured looking somewhat downcast. In the interview he would tell how failing to keep up with information technology had cost him his livelihood. Harvard's School of Business had understood the role of fear in hard-sell.

But Harvard's President, Derek Bok, resisted selling scientific research. Bok is an academic traditionalist whose wife writes books on ethics. In a 1980 speech he warned that profit motives in academe could "confuse the university's central commitment to the pursuit of knowledge and learning by introducing into the very heart of the academic enterprise a new and powerful motive – the search for commercial utility and financial gain."

But in 1989, Harvard would establish a company to license and market products of its biotechnology research. The school had already broken new ground by patenting a living creature used in cancer research, a genetically altered mouse. Now proceeds from the mouse as well as other biotech products would accrue directly to the university.

The Harvard institute was created without fanfare; the university did not even call a press conference to announce it. Perhaps that was in deference to the sentiments of President Bok. Or perhaps it was because the course of academe had turned so far toward commercialization that selling biotech no longer seemed noteworthy.

If so, there was cause for serious concern. The race toward the market-place has turned up all around the public sector, even in agencies charged with monitoring new technology. The National Institutes of Health entered into licensing agreements with a small start-up company, Genetic Therapy, partly in order to avoid losing key staff people who could earn higher salaries in private industry. Critics noted that Genetic Therapy is currently trying to win government approval of a ground-breaking experiment using human genes.

A recent National Academy of Sciences study identified the following "fields of opportunity" in scientific research: chemical and process engineering for biotechnology; high-performance polymer composites; the biology of oncogenes (tumor-producing genes); computer architecture; information technology in pre-college education; interactions between blood and blood vessels; and the biology of parasitism.

Some analysts feel that two of the disciplines underlying these fields bear watching. Leonard Slosky, a Denver-based environmental consultant, cites developments in chemistry. Today, some 65,000 chemical compounds are in commercial use. One thousand additional compounds are added each year. The effects of these compounds are global; PCBs, one form of residue, have been found in the ice cap of Antarctica.

Yet the US federal budget to monitor the effects of these chemicals has declined twenty per cent in real terms in the past decade (the same rate that defense expenditures rose). What are these chemical additives doing to us and others in the world? What will their effects be on our children? In the US, according to Slosky, we're losing the capacity to find out.

The other concern is biotechnology. The "new biology" has been building for decades and is just about to mature. Commercial application of biotechnology is still in its earliest stages. Thus far, the industry has made business headlines mostly by absorbing capital. One of the Stanford tenant firms spent $200 million in seed money over a fifteen-year period before it turned a profit. Nationwide only fifty of 400 American biotechnology firms are lucrative.

But profitable applications of biotechnology are coming on the market. Micro-organisms that devour oil-spills and digest garbage are just the beginning. Biotechnology is about to take off, and most observers believe it will out-perform computers. What will happen in the next phases of development, when biotech grows beyond the Harvard mouse?

In America one prophetic figure, Jeremy Rifkin, appears at all the hearings on government regulation. He's an abrasive individual whom industry representatives detest. But Rifkin raises valid questions. Given our history with nuclear energy, it's appropriate to ask: who will monitor the new technology? What if someone markets a method of genetically altering human beings, to make them less susceptible to carcinogens in the work place?

Or what about other technology, developed in good faith, that is insufficiently tested and goes wrong? Such as thalidomide, the sedative that caused birth defects, or the American Asian-flu vaccination program that killed or paralyzed some of those who were inoculated. Recent cardiac research at the University of Pennsylvania suggests that up to 3000 patients may have died prematurely during the past two years because two new drugs intended to prevent sudden death triggered heart attacks instead. The heart medicines, encainide and flecainide, were prescribed while tests were still under way.

History is full of similar sobering stories, even before the days of commercial high-tech. In Georgia, there's the case of the kudzu vine, a Japanese plant imported to combat soil erosion. The kudzu thrived in Georgia. In fact, it found no natural adversaries in the entire region. Today it grows rampant throughout the American South-East, engulfing whole fields and enveloping the highest trees.

Michael Crichton, the physician-writer, made the same point in his science-fiction novel, *The Andromeda Strain*. The story of a virus spreading out of control, Crichton's novel doesn't seem far-fetched today. Imagine a garbage-eating microbe running amok!

By tradition, universities have offered a kind of sanctuary where factors of social change and new technology could be carefully explored. That's why publicizing academic research in science has followed a clear set of procedures. Scientists submitted evidence for a new discovery, and made public the methods by which it was found. If the new knowledge or procedure were accepted as viable, others in the university could be counted on to question how and whether it should be used. Government bodies such as the Food and Drug Administration would then review the procedures as well.

But what is the role of the university in an atmosphere of commercial research, where knowledge is a commodity for sale? It may be different, in ways we're beginning to understand. Recently a Harvard researcher reportedly tested a non-FDA-approved commercial pharmaceutical on 100 of his patients at Massachusetts General Hospital. His medical supervisor knew of the unauthorized experiment but did nothing to stop it. It seemed that both doctors owned stock in a company that intended to market the new product.

Or there's the story of oil-shale research in Colorado. In the 1970s, Exxon, a large oil company, launched a gigantic oil-shale operation in the western part of our state. Large plants were built to extract oil from rock deposits, though the technology was still being tested. Residential communities went up as well. Local universities were flooded with requests for research proposals.

Betsy Moen, a sociologist at the University of Colorado, remembers those days. She recalls her colleagues turning bright-eyed at the sums of money Exxon offered for research. The sociology professors came up with elaborate proposals to study energy boom towns and their problems.

Then, one morning, the funding was gone. Exxon had abandoned the oil-shale industry overnight. Almost everyone outside the company seemed shocked by the decision; the economy of western Colorado is devastated to this day.

Looking back, Betsy says, there were lessons to be learned about sponsored research. "Exxon offered the university money to study every facet of oil shale except one. That was whether an industry whose net consumption of energy was greater than its output made any sense. No one was asked to consider whether the oil-shale industry itself was a good idea."

"I believe I learned this. If universities aren't encouraged to ask the most basic questions, we all had better ask: Who is?"

All the most troubling questions of academic capitalism came to a head not long ago in Utah, an out-of-the-way corner of the western United States. Utah is no stranger to controversy. It is perhaps the most anomalous, perplexing region of the country.

Parts of the state are incredibly beautiful. Driving west from Colorado through the Wasatch Range, one passes through majestic mountains and forests, and valleys so serene that it's hard to know why everyone else in the United States doesn't just pack up and move there.

The reason has a lot to do with the people who already inhabit Utah. In the last century, Utah was appropriated from the Ute Indians by the most curious cult in American religious history, the Mormons. Cast out of one community after another on their lonely pilgrimage west, the Mormons finally settled at the western edge of the Wasatch where the green mountains meet the Great Salt Desert.

Today Salt Lake City is a bustling commercial center – site of the state capital and the University of Utah. For those who love the outdoors, the city offers some of the most attractive surroundings anywhere: mountain trails and ski resorts are just at the back door. Thirty minutes east of downtown Salt Lake City, one can escape deep in wilderness.

But to most Americans the city is still a bit unnerving. At a time when other, less attractive places in the West are threatened with overcrowding, Utah's image as a bastion of Mormonism keeps a damper on immigration. Seventy per cent of the population is Mormon. So is ninety per cent of the state legislature.

Salt Lake City is about half Mormon. Much of it looks upscale and sophisticated, like any other city. There are large hotels and clothing stores, and a first-class professional basketball team. But Salt Lake City is dominated by the vision of Mormons. Downtown, their great white Temple gleams in the sun.

It's easy to prejudge Salt Lake City by the ubiquitous signs of Mormonism: their prohibition of alcohol, tobacco, and even caffeine; their historical polygamy and the value they continue to find in propagation; their derogation of black people and conditioning of women to serve men as homemakers.

Spend a weekend in Salt Lake City and, if you have a mind, the worst traces of Mormonism are all there: racism, sexism, bigotry.

There are terrible epithets toward black players from the crowd at the basketball game, absurd procedures to join a private club in order to buy a beer. The Mormon bookstore downtown features racks of mindless literature with a best seller on "saving yourself for marriage."

Non-Mormons appear mostly as reactionaries. There is an insidious, sullen underside to Salt Lake City: from defiant black teenagers blaring rap songs at the bus stop to white kids dealing drugs from an alley in the shadow of the Temple. This is street life in America's last theocracy, where people seem preoccupied either to stay within the narrow confines of Mormonism or to wrench free from it.

Utah is an unlikely place for advanced technology, to say nothing of revolutionary science. The state has a weak educational base, for one thing. A hot-bed of procreation, it has the nation's highest birthrate. With a relatively small adult population, low immigration, and natural resource industries in decline, it's hard to find adequate funds for education.

Utah ranks last among the fifty states in *per capita* expenditures for primary and secondary education. It's fortieth in funding higher education. Only half of Utah's young people complete high school, and I'm told that half of those graduates are functionally illiterate.

Utah is hardly the sort of place where one would turn for new ideas. But Utah is a venturesome state, founded by courageous non-conformists. It's a culture that understands pioneers. Utah is a place of vision.

In 1972, Utah built one of America's first ten university-related research parks, and state officials set out in search of far-sighted scientists. Their best success came in bio-engineering, where William DeVries and Stephen Jacobson developed a world-class research center.

DeVries made history in 1982 when he implanted a Jarvik-7 artificial heart in the chest of a dentist who was terminally ill. Barney Clark survived less than four months, and DeVries was subsequently lured to another venture in Kentucky. But Utah acquired a new image to offset Mormonism. Here was Bionic Valley, prosthetics capital of the world.

Martin Fleischmann is a latter-day nomad who found his way to Utah as a scientific pioneer. Fleischmann is an inveterate roamer. As a child, he emigrated from Austria to England where he excelled in school and went on to become a noted chemist. Fleischmann earned fame as an innovator. According to one British colleague, ninety per cent of his ideas are impractical; the other ten per cent are brilliant.

Fleischmann retired early from the University of Southampton and set out to teach in North America, in Michigan and then in Edmonton, Alberta. He kept in touch with a former graduate student, B. Stanley Pons, and once a year would visit his friend.

Bobby Stanley Pons is the scion of a well-to-do family in North Carolina. A bright young man with a gift for science, he made his way slowly into that profession, interrupting his graduate studies at the University of Michigan to take on management of various family businesses.

When he finally freed himself of family responsibilities, he found that American schools looked askance at the break in his studies. They required that he re-do all his graduate courses before enrolling for his doctorate. He chose to circumvent the American system by earning his degree at the University of Southampton instead.

Pons found his way to a teaching position at the University of Utah and later became chairman of the chemistry department there. In the course of his own research, he happened to generate some findings that seemed to corroborate one of the electrochemical experiments of Fleischmann.

The next time Fleischmann came to visit, Pons shared the results with his old mentor and friend. Both were absorbed by the notion of generating energy through the fusion of hydrogen atoms at room temperature, rather than relying on the multi-million-dollar devices physicists used to duplicate the intense heat of the sun.

Cold fusion was one of those abandoned paths in the history of science that are summarized in survey courses but no longer explored. Fleischmann and Pons were intrigued by the possibility that something of value might be found there. They pondered the subject on a long drive back to Salt Lake City from a conference in Texas, and continued the discussion on a hike up Millcreek Canyon. Later, on Pons's kitchen table, they put together a research plan.

For five years the chemists pursued their experiments with room-temperature fusion. They worked surreptitiously. Whether because the concept was so exploratory, and/or because of their concern for proprietary rights, they applied for no grant funds and kept their work from colleagues.

Ultimately, however, as they began to achieve some success, news of Pons's and Fleischmann's work leaked out. The chemists were by no means ready to share their work with the larger scientific community through traditional channels. Publishing a refereed article in a scholaly journal would require conducting a control experiment and formulating an explanatory theory to account for their results. The scientists hadn't had time for that. They were content to pursue their experiments at their own pace, out of the limelight in Utah.

But others at the university were not. James Brophy, Vice-President for Research at the University of Utah, was responsible for securing legal rights to anything discovered there. Brophy became uncomfortable when he began receiving inquiries about the chemists' work from scientists around the country.

Then Brophy learned of other research in cold fusion, by a group of physicists at Brigham Young University in Provo, Utah, only forty-five miles away. Officials from the two schools met to explore arrangements for jointly publicizing their efforts. Room-temperature fusion held truly revolutionary prospects of inexpensive non-polluting energy, not to mention untold economic benefits to the state.

Utah officials were exultant at the prospects of a scientific breakthrough that could dwarf the Jarvik heart. "We don't want to lose this," said a spokeswoman for Governor Norman Bangerter. "We don't want this to get out of Utah."

"If this thing is what they think it is, it's better than the gold rush," the Governor himself proclaimed.

But Brophy had allegiance narrower than Utah. Donations for fusion research were already being targeted to the University of Utah, an institution where half the payroll comes from non-tax sources. The university's vice-president for development received one gift for $100,000 and the offer of another for a million dollars. "This is better than football!" he cried.

Brophy was a prominent advocate of commercialized research. In a 1987 fund-raising booklet he'd written: "Ingenuity, inventive spirit and entrepreneurial drive are nurtured at the University of Utah through 'academic capitalism,' a philosophy that is shaping the economic future of Utah and the Intermountain West . . . a catalyst for economic development through the application of new technology, innovation and commercialization."

Brophy introduced Fleischmann and Pons to the university's patent attorneys. The lawyers reviewed an array of legal issues: "first to invent," "first to file," "constructive reduction to practice." This last provision allows someone to file for a proposed application of a discovery even before it's developed. If the application succeeds, its inventor receives patent rights after the fact.

Japanese firms had filed 200 of these conceptual patents in the aftermath of an IBM breakthrough in superconductivity, and the corporation had lost extensive rights to its own discovery. Utah's Attorney General Paul Van Dam allocated $500,000 in state funds to cover every possible angle of fusion rights.

At length the chemists were persuaded by their lawyers to publicize their work on the basis of a legal rather than scientific timetable. A press conference was held the day before a scheduled mailing of a joint article with Brigham Young.

This was not the first time such an announcement had been made through the press rather than a scientific journal. When the first laser was constructed in 1960, it was publicized in the press. So was the major superconductivity breakthrough in 1987. In both instances, scientists revealed their results ahead of schedule, to head off competitors. It was an erosion of the procedure by which science had traditionally progressed.

But the Utah announcement caused a greater ruckus. Was that a sign of prejudice? Chase Peterson believed that it was. It's another sign of "the Utah effect," he said. Intellectuals were simply biased against the state. But most scientists had other objections. The findings were very preliminary, for one thing. In the earlier cases, of lasers and superconductivity, researchers had independent corroboration of their results. Their work was much further along.

More than that, the scientists resented Utah's withholding of information on basic procedures, leaving other researchers to fumble in the dark. That's not the way of the scientific community, they said.

As the weeks of controversy went on, it seemed that the losses cut much deeper than protocol. It wasn't just the research procedures: testing evidence and publishing papers. There was a loss of spirit as well – the plain curiosity and basic excitement where so much scientific truth is born. If basic research were reduced to marketplace dimensions, something about the scientific community itself was at risk. We all could lose the truths that might be found in unconventional questions, in the kind of wild notion you might share with a trusted friend on a cross-country drive or a hike up a back canyon, the truths that need time for reflection, and ideas that require quiet space.

Can we come up with a better place to take counsel on the future than the university? It's not clear that we can. We still seem to need an impartial institution invested in truth: legitimate universities, not just profit centers selling research for funding by default; not just a joint venture of patent attorneys and academic entrepreneurs.

It seems we need universities with a sense of heritage – not the musty old ivory-tower tradition for its own sake, but an appreciation of their own historic role and place.

It appears there is a new sense of tradition at Stanford. Some of it is obvious enough: the garage at 367 Addison Avenue, where graduate students William Hewlett and David Packard developed their first invention for Walt Disney's film *Fantasia*. The garage has been nominated as a registered national historic landmark.

But most of the historic sense is more subtle. It may be just a rising appreciation for what has transpired here in the past half-century: a sense of history being born.

There's David Beach and the Norris Clock. Someone pointed him out through the window of the small, two-story monument where the clock is housed. Beach was winding the mechanism of the Norris Clock furiously when I first saw him. He spun a two-foot crank like a piston rod, churning like a dervish. Five minutes later I looked back and he was still at it. I'd never seen a campus custodian work at anything that hard.

I walked over to the door of the monument and waited till he was done. Sweating profusely, he finally uncoupled himself from the Norris Clock and rested against it. The ungainly machine was as long as a car.

Panting, he told me the history of the clock. It had hung above Old Main till the earthquake of 1906 demolished the tower. The clock had been stored away and restored several times, even though its technology has been obsolescent for more than eighty years. The last restoration was in 1983, and whoever had hooked up the mechanism to the hands had done it wrong. Now it's necessary to climb up and adjust the hands after each winding, several times a week.

I asked Beach how long he'd had this job, and wasn't surprised to learn he's not a janitor, but a professor of mechanical engineering at Stanford who winds the clock as a volunteer. "I'm the university crank," he said. It occurred to me to ask why he put himself through this. But something in his manner told me he just cared about the Norris Clock and its place in the history of Stanford. After a few moments he caught his breath and bounded up a ladder to set the hands.

Alf Brandin spoke to us after lunch from the edge of a large tent that covered the buffet. He is a burly man with broad shoulders and thick, foreboding eyebrows turning white.

Brandin played football at Stanford and was All American twice. Then he went off to World War II. Returning from the South Pacific, he remembers everyone making plans as the war drew to an end. "What are you going to do?" they all asked incessantly.

Alf returned to Stanford and became business manager of the university. He was a major figure in the birth of Stanford's research park, cutting deals with industrialists and start-up inventors all over northern California.

Now he recounted that history, from his podium at the edge of the tent, and he went on much too long. It was hard for him not to tell us the details of every transaction, to elaborate traits of people who belonged to another time.

Yet somewhere in the midst of his reminiscence, Alf Brandin's talk strangely began to come alive. It was nothing he had to say, but rather something about his surroundings. Suddenly it seemed there was a new presence in the air. A spirit of some kind had joined him.

The spirit was elusive. It might have been the sunlight, glinting on the eucalyptus leaves, shining off his forehead. Shadows streaked the creases of his graven face.

But there was something more here as well. It appeared that Alf Brandin had found a setting for his stories. As the sun passed above him, his memories seemed sheltered in the California afternoon. Now Brandin fused with the sunlight and the trees. His countenance, all dappled in shadows, reflected a spirit that lives here. Its presence would inspire whatever he had to say.

As the talk went on, Alf Brandin receded back among the shadows of this verdant campus he helped to create. It seemed that they belonged together. He, and his history, and Stanford all were one.

10 · *Coming Home*

There is a quiet spirit at work in the world. But like all living spirits, it's difficult to see. Spirits are notoriously elusive. Generally, they appear only in those penumbral places where the pace of life slows down a bit and the forces that empower it seem real.

Most often when the quiet spirit appears, I miss it. Because of my values, I'm busy looking at other places. That's a common human dilemma. We're all taught to sort out the abundant spirits of life through the lenses of specific values in order to give life focus. Anyone who fails to learn that grows up schizoid. The rest of us simply lose the value of other perspectives.

The American writer Norman Cousins tells the story of Ferdinand Magellan, the Portuguese navigator, on Cape Horn. It seemed that when the Portuguese first encountered the Indians of Tierra del Fuego, the natives were astonished to find Magellan and his soldiers in their midst. Where on earth had they come from?

Magellan pointed to the great sailing ships that lay anchored far out in the harbor, and the Indians peered to the horizon. But they could not see the ships. Those giant sailing vessels were beyond the Indians' imagination. They couldn't conceive them as anything but clouds, till the Portuguese rowed them out to climb on board.

The values through which we've learned to view the world are somewhat intransigent. That's because we learn them as children from others who were taught those values when they were young, too. Our most potent values are not perspectives we've chosen. Whenever we try to re-evaluate the values we have learned, we can expect our progress to be arduous and slow. Re-learning values is the spiritual equivalent of getting fitted with new glasses.

Nonetheless, values do change over time. From Homer to Jesus to the Age of the Smart Machine, masses of people have modified their views of the world and gone in search of different spirits. Perspectives on work have changed radically throughout the course of Western civilization.

For most of Christian history, right up through the time of Martin Luther, work was viewed mostly as a matter of necessity. Jesus was a carpenter, Paul made tents, and Adam tended the garden. Working was just part of life.

Luther was the last medievalist when it came to the Christian value of work. He believed that people ought to be content in whatever occupation they might find themselves. Work was a limited, less-than-glamorous part of the daily round. One might just as well make the best of it.

John Calvin, in the sixteenth century, took a radically different view that we have come to identify as the Protestant work ethic. Calvin represents the rising European middle class – riding the crest of an expanding economy, exploring every corner of the world. Calvin saw work in a new light: not as a limited part of life, but as a way to overcome some of life's most nettlesome limitations, such as doubt about one's worth and salvation.

Calvin, John Wesley, and other Protestant leaders encouraged Christians to work with heart and soul. "Gain all you can," urged Wesley. "Save all you can. Give all you can!" This ethic of growth and gain gave people a new way to define and affirm themselves. And it fitted hand in glove with an age of economic expansionism.

Today, however, we may be living through the death throes of the Protestant ethic. For we find ourselves in the presence of some impressive new limits, and there's reason to believe that the age of expansion is done. All of our environmental crises seem rooted in rampant human expansiveness, for one thing. That spirit has contributed to a doubling of the world's population and a quadrupling of its economic activity in the last forty years.

Yet most Western societies continue to function as though such harsh facts were not real. We proceed with business as usual in the US, raising highway speed limits even as our domestic oil runs out and we're forced to rely more on imports.

Part of our denial results from a blind faith in technology.

However we may find ourselves threatened – from dwindling energy sources, to epidemics of sexually transmitted disease, to rank starvation – we continue to seek solutions in new and more elaborate technology.

Our fundamental hope and faith lie in the human capacity, demonstrated over several centuries since the days of Calvin, to modify nature. That's why we lurch after new technologies: from superconductivity to cold fusion to whatever turns up next. We believe in progress through technology.

We believe in our own progress as well. That's much of the miasma that clouds life-at-work for so many people today. In the US, through a litany of advertisements, the American Dream is drummed into us as never before. "If you're not moving up, you're falling behind." "Who says you can't have it all?"

The other day I was talking with a young woman after a speech I'd given at a downtown Denver hotel. She was a bright, ambitious economist who was unhappy with the course of her career. There simply weren't enough jobs in Colorado for people with her training.

All her life she'd followed her parents' advice and worked hard to get ahead. They had always encouraged her to get an education. Still it seemed she couldn't progress. To make matters worse, it appeared more and more unlikely that she would even attain her parents' standard of living. What was happening to America, she wondered. Why were we falling behind in the global race?

As we visited I found myself gazing around the vast lobby of the Westin Hotel: forty-foot ceilings with crystal chandeliers, ornate tapestries on mahogany walls. A friend of mine from Kenya had been put up in this hotel last year on a government-agency tour. I'd wondered what he'd thought of all this opulence.

I decided to share what I was thinking. "What about the nations that were gaining on us?" I asked as gently as I could. Didn't it seem just that the Taiwanese should improve their standard of living? Couldn't we afford to give up a bit of this grandeur?

The economist was ambivalent. Intellectually, she agreed with me. Perhaps we ought to fall back a bit in the race. But personally it hurt. She'd been raised to value upward mobility. That was how she saw the world and evaluated her own position in it. Given those values, she acknowledged, all she really could perceive in this economy was her own failure and pain.

There are, of course, alternatives to the Protestant ethic: other spirits we might follow, had we the values to perceive them. There's the dead man ethic I'd offered the economist. For conscientious people in a privileged class, that value always makes good, rational sense.

Whatever it is you're accustomed to consuming, according to the dead man ethic, your duty is to do it less. That's the way to redress the world's inequities. The problem is that just cutting back – living less of a life – is not a very inspiring goal. After all, what can you do less of than a dead man? I understood the young economist's frustration.

Or, there's the value of life in balance. I remember a story I heard long ago from Virgil Elizondo, a Mexican-American priest who directs a Catholic Chicano studies center in San Antonio, Texas. Elizondo has spent years exploring the cultures of native Mexicans and Hispanics in the United States. He's devoted his life to helping these transplanted Latin Americans understand their ancestral culture. And of course he's interested in his own roots as well.

On one of his trips to Mexico, Elizondo came upon a group of artisans dismantling a stand where they had been selling their wares. It was 2:00 in the afternoon. "*Por que*?" he'd asked them. "Why are you closing down at this hour?"

"Why not?" they replied. "Can't you see how much we've sold? We've earned what we needed. Now it's time to go home."

I believe that's the way most people viewed economic activity prior to the Protestant ethic that took root during the Reformation. It was a holistic view of working. Economics and employment were understood as components of a balanced life. We can find traces of that outlook in the etymology of our English language. "Economics" is derived from the Greek *Oikonomia*: householder. "Employment" originally meant involvement.

That's not to say we've not always had people devoted to growth and gain. Jesus often ridiculed the effects of wealth on people: the farmer whose barns overflowed, bent on building more barns; the rich man squeezing into heaven like a camel through the eye of a needle; Dives sweltering in hell, envying Lazarus.

The people he held up as models were the *am ha 'arets*, the people of the land, sometimes poorly translated from Aramaic as "the meek" or "the humble." Those common folk seemed less subject to greed and grandiosity. They worked to live, not vice versa.

There is a short scene in the Gospel of Luke that suggests Jesus' approach to working life. He is sitting in a boat with Peter and some other fishermen, just offshore, and lending an ear to their troubles.

Peter and the others have had a frustrating day. They've been out fishing for hours, and no one has caught much at all.

Jesus, the carpenter, apparently had some knowledge of fishing as well. Work roles weren't so specialized back then, and a person could offer more than one skill.

"Try again," Jesus advised his friends. Go out deeper for a catch. That's employment as involvement. If you're unsuccessful in your work, go deeper into the problems you're trying to address. And if you need help, be sure you turn to a committed friend: the kind who's in the same boat with you.

If we understand employment as essentially involvement with others, then success becomes a matter of venturing deeper with them – not rising higher alone. Now and then I'd noticed signs of that value among my career-counseling clients, even as they struggled to survive in a difficult economy. I saw glimmerings of an ethic of involvement.

There was the elementary teacher who was fatigued from a series of personal problems, and came to me when she began to experience burnout in the classroom as well. Nonetheless she'd found herself spending twenty hours a week tracking down an abused child whose family had moved to another state. Determined to find help for the little girl at her new school, the teacher discovered that she had grown through her own suffering. She was drawn now to a new career in student services.

There was the British professor in the United States who grew up in an aging industrial city where unemployment is twenty per cent. In mid-life he tired of academic research and took up international marketing. Then, as he worked in marketing, he discovered an opportunity to establish a factory back at his birthplace, and that became the focal point of his new career.

And then there was one of my most difficult cases. He was a middle-aged man who had lost his house and savings in a divorce, sold his farm implement business, and left the crumbling rural economy of his small town only to be buffeted around our large city. Several months before when I had tried to assist him he was bitter and defeated, miserably employed in sales; it was hard to know how to help him.

Then one day he called in a renewed spirit to discuss a business venture. What he had in mind was a consulting service for small business planning. The service would be founded, he explained, on his own experience as an entrepreneur, helping others determine whether they should try to start a business of their own. It would be a way, he commented quietly, of offering others the kind of help he himself had needed.

As I was watching these people seeking work that linked their own needs with those of others, I happened to see a television interview with an elderly black deacon in a storefront church. He spoke of his work distributing food to the poor of Chicago. "It's my ministry," he said. "I guess God must have intended for me to do this kind of work, because I feel blessed in doing it."

11 · *Centering Down*

Colorado inspired a different sort of ethic of involvement. It was an irreverent form of a value one hardly expected to see in the American West at all. This region is famous for its transiency. Two-thirds of the people who live in Colorado have moved here from somewhere else. That's about the same percentage as in California.

Moreover, three-quarters of those who come to Colorado don't stay. In some parts of the West, the rates run even higher. Nine out of ten migrants to Santa Fe, New Mexico, move on. There's a painful, rootless quality to the West – a sense of endless last frontiers.

Still, some people find themselves putting down roots and paying a price of downward mobility to do so. In Durango, Colorado – an idyllic town nestled in a mountain valley down along the Animas River – many have traded ambitious dreams for the surrounding beauty. Durango has more overeducated, underemployed workers than anywhere I know.

"We have a new civic motto," one resident told me. "Durango: the city of a hundred careers. All in the same lifetime!"

It was encouraging to hear Coloradans laughing at the vagaries of their working lives. That was much better than simply suffering the frustrations of living in a state where there were far too many professionals.

In Denver, they told the story of an attorney who found he had a leaking pipe and called a plumber. The plumber fixed the pipe in twenty minutes and presented a bill for $60.

"Sixty dollars!" the lawyer exclaimed. "That's $180 an hour. Why, I'm a lawyer and I don't even charge that much. I'm appalled!"

"I don't blame you a bit," the plumber replied. "When I was a lawyer I didn't charge that much either."

Then there was the bumper sticker in rural Colorado: "Work is for people who don't know how to fish." Signs of a new ethic.

"Think globally, act locally." That was another familiar bumper sticker in America. Last summer I noticed the slogan on a postcard in a London bookstore and bought one for my office wall. It was uplifting – another indication of a world becoming one. When I got home I found it had been printed in New York City.

Sometimes I look up from my work and ponder that card. I wonder whether it might not need some revision. Maybe "Think globally, look locally, then act as best you can." My travels have taught me that the moving spirits of our day can be found almost anywhere in the world, and that the best place to address them may be at home.

Denver, Colorado is something less than a world-class city. We're a bit isolated out here in the West, in a Mountain Time Zone that encompasses a fourth of America's land mass but only five per cent of its people. London or Toronto this is not.

Yet for those with eyes to see, it seems we're as much a global epicenter as one could ask for. From questions about the value of work to the impact of advanced technology, all the spirits of our time are contending here.

Sixty miles south of Denver, at the foot of the Rocky Mountains in Colorado Springs, Seymour Cray is hard at work on his latest supercomputer. Cray is a reclusive genius who invented the high-speed computer and leads the world in its development.

Back in Chippewa Falls, Wisconsin, where he came from, it's said that Cray designed a new sailboat every year just as an intellectual exercise. He'd build the boat, then destroy it at the end of the summer so that he could start afresh the following year. Cray lives for innovation.

Thanks to Seymour Cray, America has enjoyed a leading edge in the supercomputer industry. His machines can process massive amounts of data from several sources simultaneously, and at world-class speed.

But sure enough, the Japanese have made up the slack. A new product from NEC is outperforming Cray's supercomputers by nanoseconds. Now Cray has reorganized his company and assembled a crack force of 200 technicians in Colorado Springs. They'll combat the Japanese scientists head-to-head.

Summer is a glorious season in Colorado and a wonderful time to be out on the mountain lakes. It's said that Seymour Cray's wife persuaded him to move out here because of the natural beauty. I wonder if Cray is enjoying the scenery this year, or if the sailboat succumbed to the supercomputer race.

Colorado could be a pacesetter in gaining new perspectives on economic change and finding new work values. It's the perfect setting for a post-Protestant ethic. One can cultivate all sorts of interests outside paid employment and build a balanced life here. Yet we're pressured by the same questions others face all over the world, and as preoccupied as Seymour Cray. It's hard to let go of our problems.

Like most modern cities, Denver has its share of dying industries. Most of them involve heavy manufacturing that probably didn't belong in this environment in the first place.

Rocky Flats is a plutonium-trigger manufacturing facility on the northwest outskirts of the city. The plant has been targeted by peace activists and environmental organizations for decades. There is evidence that radioactive materials from Rocky Flats have found their way into the surrounding environment; cancer rates in the immediate vicinity appear to be higher than normal.

In addition, there is continuing controversy over the disposal of nuclear waste. The neighboring state of Idaho has refused to accept any more of the toxic material. A new disposal facility in New Mexico is still under construction, and an object of protest down there.

Monitoring Rocky Flats has reached the level of military reconnaissance. One agency of the US government, the Federal Bureau of Investigation, has begun filming the plant by night with ultra-red-light surveillance devices. They're spying on another federal agency, the US Department of Energy, which oversees the plant. Recently 75 FBI agents staged a dramatic raid on Rocky Flats, seeking evidence of unreported toxic spills. The factory is an unfailing source of local headlines and high drama.

Everyone in Colorado knows that sooner or later, and certainly within a decade, Rocky Flats will be shut down. But no one knows what to do with the 5100 workers currently employed there. Most of the employees have few transferable skills and no one has come up with a plan to retrain them. It's an experienced staff with an average salary of $50,000 a year.

What will the Rocky Flats workers do if they can't make plutonium triggers? In an economy already reeling from the loss of oil and gas jobs, even the prospect of considering that question seems overwhelming. I called the personnel director to propose an advanced retraining program a few months ago. She cried, "Why don't they just leave us alone?"

There is a new economy rising in the West, concurrent with the loss of the old one. Part of it is based on efforts to rid the environment of the harm that has already been done. Hazardous waste management could become an emerging industry in the West. The many geologists who still live in this area have good basic skills for retraining in environmental analysis and waste disposal.

Furthermore, the fragility of our own arid environment constantly highlights the dangers of pollution. We're in much the same position as Canada, where structural engineers developed construction skills in harsh environments. Now Canadian firms market wilderness-engineering services all over the world.

In hazardous waste management, as in so many other new industries, the key ingredient is training. Many of the Rocky Flats workers could be trained in the new skills needed just to clean up the landsite when the plant is shut down.

But retraining is easier said than done. All sorts of older workers all over the world are overwhelmed by the technology that is revolutionizing their fields. British labor unions fight over one government training scheme after another as the old apprenticeship programs based on established crafts break down.

Others just give up. Last year, assembly-line workers at a Detroit General Motors plant were offered forty hours retraining, on company time, to prepare for technological changes in their present jobs. Seventy-five per cent of the workers were so intimidated by the new technology that they turned the training program down.

That's not entirely surprising. The scope and pace of technological change today are mind-numbing. In the US, the entire field of auto mechanics was transformed by electronics technology in just a few years. Arab oil embargoes and air pollution led to a wave of federal regulations. As a result, the auto industry was driven to introduce technology that had sat on the shelves for decades. The change to on-board computers was enormously successful; cars now get twice the gas mileage of twenty years ago, with much less pollution.

But the nation's auto mechanics were unprepared for the change. Few of them had any knowledge of electronics and physics on which the new technology was based. Today the American automobile servicing industry is in turmoil. Thousands of mechanics are losing their jobs even as thousands more are needed. By the end of the century an estimated one million mechanics trained in automotive electronics technology will be required. The shortage already is so severe that some of the best auto service technicians in Denver are making $100,000 a year.

Retraining is not just a blue-collar problem. Corporate personnel specialists estimate that fifty per cent of computer technology sold for "office automation" in the US goes unused, simply because American workers haven't learned to run it.

Last year in Denver the telephone company bought a computer software program to help managers process financial data for daily reports. The software was expensive but necessary for the kind of instantaneous data management the company needs. Yet a year after installation, twenty-five per cent of the program goes unused. Very few of the managers have been able to master a critical single-stroke key function.

Shoshana Zuboff and other industrial psychologists have begun to probe the effects of computers in the work place while seeking solutions to the problems of technical training. Zuboff spent five years studying eight corporations that were introducing computers to their operations. She interviewed top management and hourly employees, sometimes working alongside them to find out how the computers were changing their jobs.

Zuboff concluded that the effect of computers depended on their uses, for automation and/or information. Automation involved simply mechanizing routine operations: a process that usually eliminated low-skill jobs. Most firms' involvement with computers ended there.

But other companies learned to use the elaborate data computers provided to enhance their organizations. They created new products and services based on changing consumer needs, commodity prices, and market conditions. Organizations with such information became more enlightened – better connected to the complexities of a changing world, not merely more efficient.

The question of "informating" or automating organizations had a double-edged impact on employees. Workers were involved both as cause and effect. On the one hand, using computerized information depended upon training. If employees could become comfortable enough with computers to grow with the new technology, their organization could develop and their jobs would be likely to become more challenging as well.

On the other hand, if workers lacked the opportunity and ability to learn new skills, they would be likely to lose some of their old ones. For computers would be used for automation alone. In which direction was our economy heading? Will computers enhance the new work place or diminish it? Labor economists have joined in a "deskilling, reskilling debate."

It isn't hard to find evidence for each scenario. Recently I called an electronic box-office in Denver, for tickets to a concert. The clerk found two seats in Section 304. I asked where the seats were in relation to the stage. It seemed he had no idea. The computer told him only that those were the two best seats available.

That was a deskilled job. Someone had programmed a computer to perform the kinds of judgments human beings once made: scanning charts and recommending seat location. It was the kind of task that might feel rewarding and even earn a "thank you."

The new process was much more efficient than pondering a seating chart and describing various options over the phone. But it reduced the quality of someone's job and diminished the service provided. I began to notice how often I heard the same phrase from customer service representatives: "The computer says . . ."

Just as computers were accelerating service delivery, those delivering the services were evaluated on the basis of speed. The director of training at an express-mail company told of a system his company had established to evaluate customer service personnel. Representatives were measured by the amount of time they spent on the phone with customers; the less time the better. When stuck with a difficult customer, clerks were instructed to agree with their complaints, try quickly to find their missing package, and if that didn't work then refer them immediately to a supervisor.

One of the clerks, a former school teacher, found herself bored by this regimen after only a few weeks on the job. She dared not talk with a client at any length, nor tackle a complex problem, because of the emphasis on speed. Before long, however, she invented a solution.

The ex-teacher found a second phone for her desk, with another extension. Then, when a customer needed referring, she transfered the call to the second phone and answered it herself in the role of supervisor. When her scheme was discovered several weeks later, the new training director rewarded her ingenuity and scrapped the old rapid-fire evaluation system.

Yet other jobs were enhanced by computers. Not long ago, someone told me about a call he'd made to his insurance agent. Time was, he said, that whenever he had a claim or a question about his coverage, he'd have to call the agent's secretary to schedule an appointment two weeks in advance.

But recently when he called, the secretary herself was able to find the information he needed through her desktop computer. She answered his question on the spot. Now the agent spends more time on risk analysis, damage appraisals, and developing new business. The secretary has become a "Certified Professional Service Representative." Both of them have reskilled, computer-enhanced jobs.

What is the future of employment in an information-based economy? In which direction are today's jobs going? In her study of computerizing companies, Shoshana Zuboff concluded that the question is still unresolved and that the primary factors at work are political.

History is replete with instances of jobs that gain or lose skills as organizations change. The role of secretary was once a highly responsible position, often an entrée to management. But as businesses became more complex during the industrial era, the tasks of the secretary were subdivided. Chief executive officers (male) assumed the more creative tasks such as composing correspondence. Clerks (female) took on the more mundane responsibilities such as taking dictation.

Her findings rang true to me. In consulting with organizations and counseling individuals who have become unemployed, I've often seen office politics entangle new technology. There was the secretary whose new boss got her to teach him the office computer system, then fired her as soon as he could run it himself.

Or the high-tech company faced with a lay-off where the electrical engineers organized to short-circuit the work of mechanical engineers, assuring that they would be the ones let go. "Using information technology as a competitive weapon" was a skill that didn't seem to require a Harvard Business School curriculum.

No one is more vulnerable to technological change than middle managers. Not long ago I had lunch with a couple of managers at a large aerospace company. Several months before, I'd attended a demonstration of their firm's new computer graphics technology.

The equipment was impressive. I watched entire teams of engineers work simultaneously on a common design project. Each individual's work appeared in the computer graphic design in a different color. Errors and adjustments could be identified immediately.

But the managers were contending with long-established procedures for making changes in design projects, and they found the new program disconcerting. In the past, when a problem was discovered, an engineer went back to his office to write a report. He described the problem, then recommended a solution, with a requisition for additional materials and other resources. Then the report was reviewed by higher-level managers who gave their own recommendations before some ultimate superior approved it.

"What sense does that make, if everyone now can see the problem on the screen in the first place?" I asked.

"None at all," they lamented. "We know that all our competitors in France, China, Russia, and Japan now have this same computer graphics capability. We believe they're taking full advantage of it while we keep playing this ridiculous charade of writing up reports.

"The problem is what to do with all these senior managers who have spent their lives working up to the position of report-reviewers. It's clear their jobs are redundant. But then we get to thinking: maybe ours are, too."

Today's global economy is full of people like the superfluous middle managers. Most of them are devastated when their occupations turn obsolescent overnight. Sometimes I wish we could just declare a moratorium on technological change, and give everyone a chance to catch up.

Of course that's not likely to occur, nor should it. Vast sectors of our passing economy are dying for good reason. We've all benefited from the new electronic automotive technology. On-board computers have reduced toxic automobile exhaust emissions. And in Denver we'll be better off when Rocky Flats is behind us.

But we could do more to help people prepare for new developments

– perhaps at least establish some conferences where we all could consider technological change in phases: *awareness* of new technology, *assessment* of its value to us, and only then *acquisition* of new skills and equipment.

But most of all we need a work environment that encourages growth. The introduction of computers is a litmus for the capacity of co-workers to learn together – managers caring about workers whose skills are becoming obsolescent, workers daring to enter the *terra incognita* of retraining, and everyone envisioning the outcomes of change. It's clear that those benefits affect more than the quality of individuals' jobs; they reach to the heart of the organization as a learning community. The question, of course, is how to create that kind of climate.

Technical training is a burgeoning profession in most industrialized parts of the world. In the United States, the rate of growth is phenomenal. American private industry now spends more instructing employees than all our states together spend for higher education.

Last year, the National Society for Performance and Instruction held a conference of 1600 industrial psychologists and trainers in Denver. I was curious about how they were coping with technological change and took the opportunity to write a column on their field.

The conference displays offered a cornucopia of new educational material. "Principles of Technology" is a secondary-school level course in applied physics for workers such as auto mechanics who need to retrain in mid-career. Similar courses are being developed in basic mathematics and communication.

There is an array of new technology to help adults pursue independent study – the way that most of them learn best. One of Denver's cable television companies now broadcasts college courses over idle channels in the dead of night. Students can set their video cassette recorders to receive the material, then view it at their leisure. The television company procures courses from a consortium of nine universities, and performs all the traditional administrative functions: distributing texts, collecting tuition, supervising tests, and awarding grades. A new home-study MBA program was introduced this year.

Video laserdisk programs offer students immediate feedback in their instruction: another effective teaching tool. One can respond to a foreign language phrase, or a technical procedure, and immediately see the results. Pilots-in-training can visualize approaches to various airports or watch a miscue end in a crash, all without leaving the classroom.

Many of the newest video programs don't even require typing skills. Scientists have come up with a special heat-sensitive television screen that viewers can activate by touch. There's an incredible range of new developments in high-tech instruction.

Deborah Stone is a typical industrial training specialist with a graduate degree in cognitive psychology. Her firm creates customized programs to help employees learn new technology in any of thirteen different modes of learning, based on an assessment of their individual strengths and styles. From her perspective, technical training seems an exercise in human engineering.

But she happened to tell me a story about another, softer segment of the field. We'd been reminiscing about her brother, Steve Stone, a baseball player whom I remembered from my years as a sports fan in Chicago.

Steve was an exceptionally intelligent athlete who wrote poetry during his playing days and later became a successful television broadcaster. But he was no great shakes as a pitcher. In the course of eight or ten years in the major leagues, he lost as many games as he won.

Then he discovered guided imagery, a meditation technique from Eastern religious traditions. Steve devoted himself to the practice, learning to quiet his senses and slow his breathing. He concentrated his energies as a Zen master might do.

The following season, while his teammates were playing cards and carousing in the clubhouse, Steve Stone went off to spend an hour by himself before every game. He sat quietly and visualized how he would pitch to each batter. That year he won the Cy Young award as the best pitcher in baseball.

Deborah's story reminded me of an incident from Shoshana Zuboff's research. She had found that the best learners in one company were all workers on the night shift. That's when the politics and pressures of organizational life calmed down.

I was surprised to find the same spirit in one of the leading figures in the field of accelerated learning. Frank Clement is a research engineer who spent years at the forefront of telecommunications technology. He worked for decades at Bell Labs outside Denver and invented a number of patented devices. One of them was the computer touch-screen. Clement earned a PhD in electrical engineering and might have spent his entire career in research.

But when the American telephone industry was deregulated and forced to reorganize for a competitive market, Clement was asked to take on the unfamiliar role of technical trainer. He was assigned to a program to retrain telephone linemen as computer programmers. The phone company had engaged a private consulting firm to conduct the training, which was to be completed in only thirty-five days.

The crash course was a disaster. The consultants concentrated voluminous material in traditional lectures, and most of the employees were overwhelmed. Clement was disturbed watching the workers struggle to master a strange, complex technology. Their careers were at risk, and they were failing.

After three weeks, Clement set out on a crash course of his own. He had no formal training in education, but he was certain there must be other more effective methods of technical instruction. He set out to find them before the allotted thirty-five days elapsed.

That's how he discovered the work of Eastern European specialists in "super learning." He learned about the "right brain" and found new ways to engage that neglected hemisphere in the educational process. One method was introducing new material to a background of Baroque music, which echoes the natural rhythm of the heart.

Clement helped bring most of the telephone workers successfully through the training process. Then he went on to develop other programs that reduced instructional time by forty per cent while increasing retention by one-half. Students were able to acquire a 1000-word foreign-language vocabulary in three days, with ninety per cent retention. These were similar results to accelerated learning programs in Bulgaria, largely unknown in the United States. Clement was captivated by this work. He never returned to research.

Today, Clement operates a center for accelerated learning from his home in Boulder, Colorado. He conducts seminars for private students and travels the world as a consultant to companies installing new technology.

When I drove up to interview Clement for a newspaper column, I was surprised by the person I found. Professional seminar leaders are typically flamboyant extroverts. But Clement was a quiet, almost diffident individual who seemed a bit reluctant to talk about himself.

I became more interested in his personal development than the teaching techniques. There was a sense of quiet depth to the man. How did he get to this place from being an inventor, I wondered. Why does one trade a lifetime of manipulating physical objects and concepts for all the imprecision of teaching people?

It wasn't clear that Clement understood his own journey. He'd grown up in a very structured life. A Roman Catholic scientist with a half-dozen children, he'd devoted himself to the industrious values he'd been raised in. The PhD had simply evolved from a lifelong regimen of going to work and school.

Then in mid-life something had triggered change. It may have been his empathy for those blue-collar workers with families of their own, struggling to keep their jobs. Perhaps it was just living in Boulder, a spiritually sensitive community where the largest established religion is Buddhist.

Clement spoke haltingly about his new life. Conducting workshops around the US, flying off to seminars in the Soviet Union, it all seemed something of a puzzle to him.

"I spend a lot of time by myself back up in the mountains," he said, "it's a good place to concentrate. All I know at this point, looking back, is that in the politics of trying to get ahead at Bell Labs, I wasn't fitting in. And I began taking all this other in." He waved toward Boulder and his Buddhist neighbors: the world outside the lab.

Clement paused for a moment to take in the view. "If I have any gift at all, it's reducing complex subjects to popular form," he said. Then he fell silent again. It was a stillness deep enough to listen for echoes of vocation.

Driving back to Denver, I spent some time in silence, too. I gazed across the ranchlands at the mountains and considered what I knew about accelerated learning. It was a paradoxical business with some suspect motives, I thought. Americans' interest in the field seemed to stem from our high-technology race with Japan. In the totalitarian states of Eastern Europe, I suspected, cognitive psychology had a good deal to do with thought control. Accelerated learning seemed to have been spawned by two of the most malodorous movements of our time.

Yet I couldn't get over the humanizing side of the field – speeding up learning by centering down, teaching to the rhythm of the heart. It was the stuff of older East-West dialogues, between Christian mystics and the masters of Zen. Here was the same resilient spirit back again: persisting in the world, enduring in the midst of mindless change. Could the need to learn new technology restore us to our right minds after all? I mused along the mountains of the Front Range.

The traffic thickened near Denver and I turned my attention to the cars and semitrailers whizzing by. Soon I was caught up in the frantic swirl of the freeway. But I managed one last centered thought. I remembered the supercomputer race, further down the highway in Colorado Springs. And I hoped that Frank Clement could stay a step ahead of Seymour Cray.

12 · *Deep Growth*

The journey didn't end. Not in Colorado where our economy still reeled like a rudderless vessel, out of control. Thousands more lost their livelihood in Denver. Home loan foreclosures doubled. Even people who had work found themselves debating development strategies; the questions were impossible to ignore.

At least one industry showed signs of steady growth. That was the field of economic development itself. 10,000 Americans are now employed as economic development specialists in 8,000 agencies across the country. There are something like forty-five development agencies in metropolitan Denver alone.

Economic development is a new enterprise for state governments – an area they've entered almost by default, following cutbacks in federal appropriations. There's a frantic quality to the efforts of some states, reminiscent of Lyndon Johnson's War on Poverty: a welter of programs swirling around some serious problems whose causes aren't quite understood.

As a profession, economic development is still in its infancy; most people I know in the field are dedicated, but still feeling their way. Some of their tactics are childlike. Colorado has spent its best efforts on quick-fix solutions, in the fervid spirit of the Gold Rush. The state has come up with an array of slick promotions – free vacation trips to companies considering relocation here, mass mailings of mountain scenes complete with 3-D glasses, sending the Governor to London, where he skied down a mound of artificial ice in Hyde Park.

Other strike-it-rich schemes have targeted massive projects that every other state sought, too: the Winter Olympics (Utah won), the superconductor-supercollider (lost to Texas), the relocation of Sears Roebuck (the giant retailer remained in Illinois).

"Smokestack chasing" is an unadmirable strategy with a beggar-thy-neighbor spirit about it. Studies show that it's ineffective as well. No more than five per cent of new jobs come from corporate relocation. Pirating industries has a destabilizing influence on local economies. It undermines the deliberate planning which communities need to follow if they're to find a strategic vision of their own.

One Colorado state official told me of visiting a German company that operates a small factory manufacturing buses out in the Colorado plains. He'd been dispatched on a trade mission to see whether any other German companies might consider moving their operations here, too.

The German executive listened carefully to his visitors' sales pitch. Then he opened a drawer in his desk and pulled out a long roll of blue paper. "Do you know what this is?" he asked. "It's the architectural drawing for a building the state of Pennsylvania has offered to give us if we'll move our Colorado plant to Scranton."

Courting corporations is not just an American stratagem. One can find the same slick promotional literature in Switzerland and Scotland, perhaps from the same advertising agencies.

Of course not all recruiting efforts are futile. Sometimes they build new trade relations and garner branch plants that may bolster Third World economies. Mexico now has numerous *maquiadora* assembly plants all along the US border. One city, Tijuana, now has 70,000 jobs in the television manufacturing industry alone, and the lowest unemployment rate in Mexico.

Most of the employees are young women from rural areas who readily adapt to factory routine. By the standards of industrialized countries, theirs is not a good lot. The workers are highly regimented. They receive low wages with few rights. Organized labor is unheard-of.

Income from branch plant manufacturing jobs may make other kinds of development possible, but only in the context of an independent plan. Without a strategy for building autonomy, communities may find themselves economically colonized, sometimes within their own country.

Last summer I came across the New Mexico director of economic development at a conference near Abiquiu in the beautiful, barren highlands of that state. We sat out under the massive red mesa at Ghost Ranch, down the road from artist Georgia O'Keeffe's old place, and he spoke candidly about his field.

It turned out he'd just left his position as economic development director. Whatever the reason, it was clear that he still cared about his job. He knew that economic development was vital to a state where some mining counties had thirty-five per cent unemployment. But he was exhausted from the politics of his profession, and the reward system most of all.

"It's nothing but numbers," he complained. "We all know that what New Mexico needs is manufacturing jobs. Those jobs build an economic base and bring in real income. But building manufacturing industries takes time and money; you can create retail jobs in a chain store for a fraction of the cost. And if you want to keep your own job in economic development, that's what you learn to do. The only thing they count is the numbers."

He'd sent me up to see Tierra Wools on my way back to Denver. It's a little woolen mill and shop on the narrow main street of Tierra Amarilla, a small Hispanic town off a back road in northern New Mexico.

The cooperative was founded by Hispanic sheep ranchers to process the wool produced in their valley. They'd renovated an old brick warehouse, built looms, and trained weavers. Then they'd started a subsidiary business raising sheep dogs. Now there are a cluster of wool-related businesses and fifteen new jobs in town. They've never applied for a federal grant.

Tierra Wools is a model of the best, lasting economic development in the West. It's locally based, deliberate, and slow. I suspect that's the kind of economic life that originated around the watering holes, before the boom-and-bust cycles took hold.

Not many communities have the kind of maturity and motivation one finds in Tierra Amarilla. But there's some evidence of the same spirit in other parts of the region. As an environmental attorney in Denver commented the other day, "We may be learning not just to grow but to grow up."

Several months after my visits in New Mexico, I found myself interviewing some economic development officials in northern Colorado for a study of industrial training needs. Meeting with these local leaders, I found myself in a modest environment of basement offices, minimal staffs, and scant publicity – nothing like the high-rise suites of the large, statewide economic development organizations. None of their cities is very large. But each of them is engaged in some serious strategic planning with an interest in long-range goals.

Most of the communities are wrestling with questions of market position. They're small enough to recognize that they can't be all things to every industry; they need to build on their strengths. Several small cities seem clear enough about their own identities to collaborate with one another.

Boulder and Longmont are building an impressive high-tech industry together. Longmont is becoming a major center for manufacturing computer peripherals, trading on its small-town ambience and ties to the research facilities of the University of Colorado at Boulder. There now are a half-dozen computer-components manufacturers in "the disk drive capital of the world."

Fort Collins, Loveland, and Greeley are three small cities in a rural, northern part of the state. Together they have a population of less than 200,000. But they share a well-educated labor force – more than a third are college graduates – and that work force has attracted some large high-tech firms to the region. A good highway system enables workers to live in any one of the cities and commute to another.

The communities know they belong together. Their economic development directors meet regularly, and next fall the public officials of all three cities will hold a joint planning retreat. At the same time they appreciate their differences.

Greeley presents itself as a conservative sort of place: "Colorado's proven opportunity." Fort Collins is clear about marketing its age. When Colorado State University is in session, Fort Collins' population is ten years younger than Loveland, only seven miles away. The city is targeting telemarketing firms, an industry interested in youth.

Outside the new Civic Center in Loveland, beside the duck pond, there is a sculpture entitled "Twist of Fate." It's a large ring, linking figures from every phase of the human life-cycle, from childhood to death. There's a retirement center across the pond, between the bike paths and library. Loveland is an ambitious, growing city. But it clearly welcomes older citizens and artists as well.

There's something refreshing in the distinctiveness of these communities. They're a lot like Tierra Amarilla and other independent places where people can build on what they do best. Sometimes it seems that's what economic development comes down to. It's just finding one's place in the world.

Building an independent economic base, of course, requires more hard work and planning than philosophizing. It seems there is a kind of rationale to the process with principles we're beginning to understand. Some insightful analysts are turning up in the field.

Mike Piore is a quiet, thoughtful economist who found himself unexpectedly in demand as a lecturer several years ago. Piore is on the faculty of the Massachusetts Institute of Technology. When Massachusetts Governor Michael Dukakis' political star began to rise, so did the market value of local economists. For a time it seemed that everyone connected with "The Massachusetts Miracle" shared some cabalistic wisdom on economic recovery. Speakers' bureaus recognized an opportunity and sent them all out on the road.

I drove down to Colorado Springs to interview Piore before an evening college lecture. I'd found his most recent book, *The Second Industrial Divide*, very helpful. It's a comparison of Massachusetts' high-tech industry with the New York City garment industry where Piore grew up.

There were some striking similarities. Each industry was based on a groundwork of craft. The garment industry was an amalgam of small firms that competed for design contracts three times a year. After each round of bidding, the winning firms would hire employees off the losers. Then four months later the bidding would resume. If the losers won out, they'd employ their bosses in turn.

Piore found that in Italy and other sectors of the global garment industry the process worked the same. The rise and fall of individual firms was less significant than the pool of talent available in an area. Craft skills kept a local industry alive.

It occurred to Piore that the same sort of process was taking hold around Boston. He attended a meeting of the Venture Club, a monthly gathering of business people and inventors in a hotel out on Route 128, Massachusetts' high-tech highway. Each month, everyone picks up a nametag in one of four colors: capitalists with money to invest, entrepreneurs with new inventions or business ideas, prospective managers of new firms, and business consultants.

Just as in the garment industry, the Venture Club members formed and disassembled organizations based on new constellations of their skills. MIT had figured prominently in that process; a recent study showed that the school had been involved in 150 of 212 new companies. Now Massachusetts' high-technology industry had matured enough to regenerate a critical mass of business; the industry had a life of its own.

Out in the West there were glimmerings of the same process: growth by growing up. Some states were targeting their research and development funds to certain key industries where it seemed they enjoyed a comparative advantage. Utah had its Bionic Valley. In Kansas, where both the agricultural and energy industries had suffered, they pumped funds into a promising pharmaceuticals research program at the University of Kansas, and another to upgrade light aircraft manufacturing through advanced technology, with Wichita State University.

In New Mexico they'd come up with a way to market wasteland. Someone had researched the explosives industry and found that scientists in that field like to work in desolate regions; they prefer not to transport their experiments very far.

The New Mexico School of Mines equipped some laboratories for explosives research. Then they persuaded an executive of Nitro Nobel, the Swedish dynamite manufacturer, to relocate to the small town of Socorro. Today they're a major center of research in the thriving industry of explosives technology.

There was a compelling logic to this business of economic development. Suppose that a state, a nation, or any economic region took time for some careful strategic planning. They might ask themselves the following questions.

What's the outlook for a particular industry: Is it growing? What's the potential impact of the industry in our area? If we were to develop some of the skills and facilities that industry needs, how would we benefit? What about our impact on the industry? Do we have the capacity to add value to it?

And a few others. How well does the industry match the characteristics of our population and environment? Does it seem to fit what we can do here? Are there features of our community, such as New York City's designers or Socorro, New Mexico's desert, that lend us some sort of comparative advantage?

Outlook, impact, fit. The strategy didn't always require sophisticated resources. Omaha, Nebraska had built a thriving telemarketing industry that employed over 5,000 people. They had only two assets to offer: location in a central time zone so that one could call everywhere in the country during much of the day, and the fact that among Americans Midwesterners have no discernible accent. Customers are likely to feel more receptive to an Omahan calling up with a sales offer than a Southerner, for instance.

But telemarketing was no paradigm for economic prosperity. Most effective development was based on providing services to producers rather than consumers. That required specialized skills. The future seemed to lie with people who could grow together, building on what they do best.

Information products were a typical, promising industry in our area. For reasons that had mostly to do with geography, Colorado found itself a national center for both the cable television and telephone industries.

Cable television had grown up naturally in the West as a means of transmitting clear pictures to communities in outlying areas such as Wyoming. The industry is less than fifty years old, but has been exceptionally successful in extending its services. Today over eighty-five per cent of the United States is wired for cable reception. (The telephone industry took 100 years to cover the country.) Cable systems are proliferating in England and Europe as well.

The question now, however, is what to do with this technical capacity. Americans are not enamored of cable TV. Presently only half the capacity of the system is used. In some cities the figure is even lower. Only one household in three subscribes to Denver's cable TV services.

The industry still is dominated by telecommunications engineers – the kind of people who specialized in designing systems and laying cable. Their vision of the future is to improve picture quality through innovations such as High Definition Television (HDTV). A new industry-wide laboratory was created this year; it will be in Boulder, Colorado.

But others aren't so sure that the future lies in improving transmission. Jerry Bennington is a former college professor with degrees in electrical engineering and applied mathematics. He heads an unusual company that provides customized news information via television.

Bennington's X*PRESS Information Services, Ltd, offers continuously updated stock quotations, sports scores, and late-breaking news stories from a dozen wire services all over the world. The service is available to cable television subscribers who also own a home computer. One can designate the kind of information desired by entering certain keywords; then the system sorts out just those stories to be stored in computer memory till it's time to read them, print them out, or store them on diskette.

X*PRESS still is not an overwhelming commercial success. It's hard to identify a clear market segment. Which cable TV subscribers/personal computer owners want to follow current events all over the globe? So far the most enthusiastic users are schools, where students can track news from a certain part of the world or compare news wire stories from several different countries.

But there are strong indications that some service like this will become popular in the future, because of the problem of information overload. A recent study in *Forbes Magazine* found that the amount of data transmitted by US media has increased three times faster than the capacity of people to receive it.

Who will help us manage a burgeoning output of information? It's not clear that newspapers can. Most of them are suffering the impact of television, streamlining formats and abridging stories.

X*PRESS Information could help people to inform themselves selectively, especially if they'd carry some better material. Why not offer feature stories from *The Christian Science Monitor* or *The Times* of London, with keywords to help subscribers track certain topics at depth? It's an idea in which I've tried to interest Bennington.

Someone is certain to offer information management services. The telephone companies have their own research under way. Information Gateway, a new product similar to the French Minitel, is being test-marketed now in Omaha, Nebraska. Gateway is a creation of US WEST Advanced Technologies, the research arm of a major telephone company and successor to Bell Labs. This facility, too, is now headquartered in Boulder, Colorado.

Gateway offers information on the order of a telephone directory, restaurant and shopping guides for a local community. The product is so new that not even its appearance has been determined; no one knows whether the final model will look like a computer, a telephone, or both.

But it is clear that the present legal barriers that separate America's telephone and cable television industries will come down. New hybrid products will emerge for transmitting and disseminating information, and they'll draw on the resources of both industries.

That's one American response to Japan's colossal manufacturing conglomerates, the *zaibatsu*.

Bennington believes that cable television needs to improve in the kinds of information and entertainment content it offers, rather than just the quality of transmission. He sees the industry at a critical juncture typical of every new technology.

"First there's invention, finding out what we can do. Then there's application, which usually takes the form of replicating old products. In the early days of motion pictures, people filmed stage plays. We've been broadcasting zillions of basketball games.

"Now we're at the third stage, diffusion, where you have to use the new technology to add value and come up with something new. The music video is one example of where we've done that. It's a whole new entertainment form with unheard-of occupations such as the video jockey. We created the VJ!"

How much of the next generation in information services will come from Colorado? The answer is still untold. Certainly our traditional transiency is no asset. Most new technologies have evolved in places where people put down roots. That's how lumbering gave rise to furniture manufacturing in north central Michigan. Then as the furniture-makers experimented with curing compounds, a new chemical industry was born. Down on the Great Lakes, automobile manufacturing evolved from the marine engine industry in just the same way.

Economic development theory holds some intriguing ideas – outlook, impact, fit; invention, application, diffusion. Those are elements of a genuinely useful strategy that ought to enter other fields such as career counseling.

But in the long run, it seems, finding our place in the new economy may depend less on sophistication than perspiration. Perhaps it's like the field of public relations. As a consultant once told me, that's about as glamorous as the life of a football lineman. "It's just your basic blocking and tackling," he said, "but somebody's got to do it." More and more, I've come to believe that our global economic future will depend on our capacity to work and learn together over time.

What is it that enables people to concentrate their energies in a single time and place and invest in a common goal? I believe it's the same spirit I've seen in the Kenyan tradition of *harambee*, and in North America, too.

There's the case of Mike Riley, head coach of the Grey Cup Champion Winnipeg Blue Bombers, and one of the most popular figures in the Canadian Football League. Earlier this year, I heard that he'd been offered the position of defensive coordinator at Stanford and wasn't surprised to learn that he'd accepted.

Mike had won the Grey Cup in Ottawa last year, so the Canadian Football League offered no more worlds to conquer. Nor could one even be assured that the League would last another season. Joining a major American college athletic program was a sensible career decision.

Riley's Winnipeg players were disconsolate when he took the Stanford job. James Murphy, one of the wide receivers, dropped in on someone I know who's the team publicist, the day after Riley left. He was heartsick.

"Don't worry," said Kevin. "He'll be back."

"How do you know that?" asked a startled Murphy.

"He didn't clean out his desk."

Sure enough, thirteen days later, Riley was back in Winnipeg. Less than two weeks in the Stanford ivy, and he realized how much he missed the Manitobans back home.

"There was never any question," Kevin added. "Like I said to James, 'Mike's a small-town guy.'" Despite the fact that the city of Winnipeg is thirty times the size of Palo Alto, I remembered the warm, down-to-earth spirit of the CFL and I knew exactly what he meant. Winnipeg was a place you could call home.

There is a spirit at the heart of the global village. I'm not always certain what to call it, but I recognize its presence. The spirit that bonds us is whole, organic, and truly alive. It's a quiet spirit in the wind of change. Often I saw it most clearly in the darkness, for what it is not. The spirit runs counter to most of the dominant values of my own American culture: racing faster and rising higher to reach some other place. This spirit had more to do with deeper investment in one's own work at home.

Gathering material for my careers column, I began to notice how often those I found forming new industries and occupations did so not by changing careers themselves, but by learning to do familiar work better. They ventured deeper.

Curtis Shortridge was a disenchanted attorney. Ten years out of law school he could no longer tolerate the inefficiencies of Colorado's bloated legal system. The state's court dockets were so crowded that it was not uncommon to wait a year and a half before a case could be brought to trial.

Shortridge decided to take advantage of a new state law that requires civil cases involving damages of $50,000 or less to be sent to arbitration. The law provides for training and licensing of arbitrators with basic dispute resolution skills. Arbitrators may be assigned cases that bear on their principal professional skills. Many of them have backgrounds in real estate, construction, engineering, and medicine.

Others with a background in human services can be trained as mediators; these individuals may go beyond ruling on a conflict to help actually resolve it. Arbitration/mediation laws have proven effective in other states. During a recent year in Hawaii, eighty-six per cent of the cases brought to arbitration never went to court.

I interviewed Curtis Shortridge, his wife Pat, and a psychotherapist who practices with them in their arbitration hearing room. It was nothing like a court room. The hearing room had a decor of soothing gray, with soft lights and a low ceiling. Southwest Indian art warmed the walls. In the center of the room was a three-sided table for face-to-face communication.

The young firm is working hard to make ends meet. Colorado's new law is still being tested, and clients are uncertain what to expect from arbitration. Much of the firm's income depends on fees from Curtis's traditional legal practice.

But the work feels needed. As they communicate with clients across the triangular table, it seems they're getting down to what law was intended to be about. "When it comes to disputes," Pat Shortridge said, "we all want to be certain we're heard."

As I left the interview, I wondered whether the next frontiers of vocation might not include more environments like this. Perhaps we'll create more places where people can work on problems in learning, health, or conflict resolution and build new skills for living at the same time.

I certainly saw a growing need for dispute resolution in high-tech fields, as Mike Piore's garment district scenario took hold in Colorado. There were several local industries where firms were spinning off one another to form a critical mass. Talking with employers in disk-drive manufacturing, plastics-injection molding, cable television and telecommunications, and dental hygiene products, one could see Piore's process taking hold.

There were benefits, as he'd described. Now it was easier to recruit skilled employees such as engineers. If a job didn't work out with a Longmont computer firm, one could move to another company without leaving town. It was the same process one found in Silicon Valley where engineers average a year and a half per job.

The problem we now saw in Colorado was that when employees moved, they took their technology with them. Longmont's half-dozen computer peripheral research firms were all concentrating on a common product: the notebook computer. All the companies were growing and employees were shuttling back and forth.

A personnel director at one of the plants told me of interviewing a new employee. She offered to introduce the person to others in the company. "Oh no, I already know everybody I'm working with," the worker replied. This was the underside of grassroots economic development: the fear of incestuous competitors.

At the heart of the global village, wherever one may go, there is an inescapable intersection of personal interests. Spirits conjoin. There is the potential for conflict as well as community. There's an ineluctable need for the qualities of patience and trust for which we humans have always sought and struggled, and without which we cannot collaborate much at all.

Epilogue

Six months after we picked up seventeen computers for Kenya, they were still in Denver. We couldn't get them working. We did receive a small grant to send a computer specialist from Earlham College over to Kaimosi to install the computers and offer instruction to the faculty.

George Silver came to Denver from Earlham in Indiana and worked on the computers for two days. But we hadn't received the proper documentation and he couldn't get the settings right. Time was running out to ship them before he had to leave.

We all worked for hours on those computers. Now we were growing frustrated and tired. This might have been a foolish idea to begin with. Perhaps the Global Technology Foundation was too ambitious after all. Maybe Quakers should leave computers to the multinationals.

Then, just as our patience was exhausted, an East Coast freelance writer came out with an article on the Global Technology Foundation for an airlines magazine. He'd interviewed the operations manager at Synergen, the biotech firm in Boulder that had donated the computers.

Jim Redenbarger turned out to be the resource we needed. He's an ex-Peace Corps volunteer who understood our project and cared about what we're doing. He dug up some manuals to figure out the dipswitch settings. If that didn't work, he said, he'd send a technologist down to help us.

But of course it wasn't just technology we needed, any more than Peter needed advice on where to fish. It was a spiritual companionship, in the basic sense of feeling supported and heartened again. If we ever got these computers running, maybe we could share that sense with the Kenyans, too.

Two months later, the computers were in Kenya. But for some reason they'd not cleared customs in Nairobi. It was just a matter of time, we were told. So George and his wife set out for Kaimosi.

A couple of weeks later we received a letter. "I thought I'd let you know how things have been going during the first two weeks of the great adventure," George began.

The trip had not gone altogether well. There was a bomb scare in New York, then a missed connection in Frankfurt, a flight back to London for a five-hour wait until the next direct flight to Nairobi. A forty-four hour journey in all.

Then came the discovery that a Kenyan government official had appropriated the computers to dole out among other schools instead. George and a Friends College faculty member had enlisted the aid of a twenty-five-year-old Minister of Parliament who represented the Kaimosi area. They liberated the computers from customs and got them on a truck for Friends College.

"I have just finished my first three days at the College," George continued. "It's Saturday and I begged to be allowed to work with the computers and get some class planning done for the coming week. This is easier said than done – I have to lock the door to the lab to discourage multitudinous watchers coming in and observing my every move from a distance of about one foot. . . ."

He went on to outline a dusk-to-dawn schedule – five classes a day with thirty students and twenty members of the faculty.

"It has been exhausting. . . . But I have in three days taught the faculty all the basics of entering, editing, and printing using WordStar.

"The classes with the students are also going well. The faculty are all as bright and eager as you said they would be. I already have my eye on two or three in the tech specialist group who have all the instincts of hackers. In short, I really think that we ought to be able to pull this thing off!"

Then Simeon Shitemi wrote to describe a ceremony to commission the computers for Friends College: "This has given so much joy and promise to many people . . . The presence of George and Jane Silver was a beautiful testimony of international Quaker Cooperation . . . I wish you were present to share with us the joy of the community."

I savored those letters and pondered what we'd done. Who can tell what the outcome of our work in Kaimosi will be? Will we build new relationships as partners in new technology? Or will we simply complicate life in Kenya by contributing to its automation? It's one more enigma of the times.

Yet somewhere in the midst of all our trials with two cultures and a new technology, I recognized a strong, familiar feeling. It seemed the possibility of global community was real.

Not just in the realm of international relations: those incredible headlines from Warsaw and Prague and Berlin. Not even in the transmutation of economic systems. My experience was more personal than that. I felt a certain spirit again.

It seemed that wherever we struggle together with the technology of our times – fishing nets or networked computers – friendship may grow in the grist of that endeavour. Not from the technology itself, of course, but the exercise in pulling together: *harambee*. Those are the times worth working for, in a deep and quiet spirit that has not died.